Having hiked in the Larapinta with Kate in 2022, I had the privilege of sharing her second annual 'Go Big Goal'. So I can personally vouch that Kate is absolutely living her best 'Life List'. With our little trekking group with whom we quickly developed bonds, we experienced countless hours of talking, laughing and sweating whilst hiking, climbing and slipping or falling, as well as sitting around the campfire at night or floating down the icy Larapinta River, to reflect on life. The vision, ideas and structure Kate has developed around her own 'Life List' to help others build their own meaningful 'Life List', and more importantly to motivate us all to go out and live an audacious life, is commendable.

—Fiona Pak-Poy, Chair, Tyro Payments

Kate Christie is truly one of a kind—I've never met anyone so incredibly passionate and so hugely capable when it comes to helping people take control of their time—the number one issue we all face in life. With *The Life List*, Kate takes us to the next level with her unique formula for how to use your time to create a life by design. Kate is a bestselling author, international speaker, she's appeared on Australian and NZ television, she has been featured on radio and in print as a leading commentator on time management and living your absolute best life. Her laser-like focus is to help people take control of their time to ensure more meaningful success across career, family, community, and life. Clearly I'm a fan.

—Andrew Griffiths, international bestselling author of 14 business books (sold in over 65 countries) and global speaker

Forget sinking into comfy slacks and daytime TV. In *The Life List*, Kate Christie acknowledges middle age is a time of power, creativity and freedom. It felt like she was talking straight to me, an empty nester refusing to go quietly and wanting middle age to mean transformation and a big, meaningful life. A real life time lord, she meshes her lived experience of love and loss with her time management expertise to give a compelling fresh take on the message life is too short. Kate compels you to want to be and do everything now while you can enjoy it all. An inspirational, practical and contemporary call to action for fit, fabulous and successful

women craving adventure over comfort and wanting their next chapter to be all about them.

—**Kate Halfpenny, Bad Mother Media,** *The Age* **columnist, former executive editor** *WHO Magazine*

Kate's lived experience is a powerful reminder of why life is too short and needs to be lived fully now. *The Life List* is a step-by-step process to re-examine the life you are living and the life you want to live. Kate's honesty and humour will guide the way.

—**Kemi Nekvapil, best selling author of** *Power:*
A Woman's Guide to Living and Leading Without Apology
and host of *The Shift Series* **podcast**

Get out of my head!! From the opening chapters of this book I felt as though Kate had jumped inside my brain and swum around (poor Kate!). The idea of 'mid life' had been irksome to me for a while but I was so caught up in my own world I hadn't stopped to consider there was something I could do about it. Enter *The Life List* and voila. Light bulbs went on, ideas came stirring and a sense of order began to seed deep inside my soul. Without a doubt this is a book that every woman needs in her life. With no more fucks to give it's time we got our shit sorted and focused on the things we want while we're young enough to enjoy them. This is the book that wakes you up, empathises with you, then gives you the tools to make it happen.

—**Tracy Sheen, tech futurist and author of**
The End of Technophobia, **Australia's Business Book of the Year**
and Best Technology Book, 2021

THE LIFE LIST

THE LIFE LIST

Master Every Moment
and Live an Audacious Life

KATE CHRISTIE

WILEY

First published in 2023 by John Wiley & Sons Australia, Ltd

Level 4, 600 Bourke St, Melbourne Victoria 3000, Australia.

Typeset in Adobe Caslon Pro 11pt/15pt

© Time Stylers Pty Ltd 2023

The moral rights of the author have been asserted

ISBN: 978-1-394-18451-4

NATIONAL
LIBRARY
OF AUSTRALIA

A catalogue record for this book is available from the National Library of Australia

Cover design by Wiley
Cover and internal butterfly image: © paci77/Getty Images

Disclaimer
The material in this publication is of the nature of general comment only, and does not represent professional advice. It is not intended to provide specific guidance for particular circumstances and it should not be relied on as the basis for any decision to take action or not take action on any matter which it covers. Readers should obtain professional advice where appropriate, before making any such decision. To the maximum extent permitted by law, the author and publisher disclaim all responsibility and liability to any person, arising directly or indirectly from any person taking or not taking action based on the information in this publication.

To Freddie, Wally and Peggy—the loves of my life

Contents

Introduction

I want more moments that are spectacular

The year I turned 50 I experienced the first tantalising taste of how I could (and should) live an audacious life if I simply learned how to master every moment. I went skiing for the first time in my life. In France no less. I mean—if you are going to do life-or-death, crazy-as-bat-shit stuff in your 50s, you may as well do it right!

In all honesty, I did not want to go skiing, had never had the faintest desire to go skiing, and would not have gone skiing at all but for my daughter.

The reason I am introducing a tantalising little taste of the skiing incident up front is to foreshadow the whole Life List plot—to set the scene for exactly why and how to create your own Life List of audacious, wonderful, life-changing and singularly spectacular moments. Because, fair to say, if I'd had a Life List prior to the skiing incident, skiing would not have been on that Life List. Because I did not want to go skiing. Ever.

But skiing I went, and it changed my life. Not that it sparked a life-long, enduring passion for skiing—god no. Rather, skiing was the vehicle by which I changed my whole approach to goal setting and goal smashing. And that is why it is so critical to this story.

Skiing was the inspiration that caused me to discover the power of the word 'moment'. Where I first fully embraced the concept of living in the moment. Where I realised that I want to have many more 'moments' in my life: moments that create memories; moments where I am fully present; moments that are anything but mundane; moments that bring me joy and wonder and delight and laughter. Moments that are life changing.

On discovering my most favourite word in the world

I use the word 'moment' a lot, and have always done so quite mindlessly. Generally I use it to buy myself time with my kids when they scream '*Mum!*'

There are two inflections to that word—'*Mum!*' There is the 'drop everything and run' inflection because one of my kids has cut their leg off. And then there is the 'I don't need to drop anything at all or run, just because they can't find a spoon' inflection. For the latter, my response is generally along the lines of, '*Just give me a moment*'.

'Moment' is the word I use to buy myself time. And as a time management specialist I am all about buying time.

But what exactly does the word 'moment' actually mean?

On looking into the word properly I was thrilled to discover that it can be so much more than just a vehicle to buy me a little time to finish whatever it is I am doing before I go and show the 20-year-old where the spoons are kept.

In fact, there are three separate definitions for 'moment', and it was a combination of these three definitions that gave me the willpower, in the face of massive self-resistance, to get myself onto the ski slopes in France, and which I have continued to use to completely redesign my life.

And that's what this book is all about—a life by design. A life where you get to master every moment and live a truly audacious life.

Moment 1 — as a unit of time

First, I discovered that, rather than buying me an unquantifiable amount of time, the word 'moment' is an actual unit of time. 'Moment' first appeared in the English language in the eighth century when Saint Bede the Venerable recorded that each hour of the day is divided into four quarter hours, 10 minutia and 40 momenta — the latter representing 90 seconds of time. Just like a 'minute' is 60 seconds, a 'moment' is 90 seconds.

This tickles me pink. Next time I say, *'Just give me a moment'*, what I am actually doing is buying myself exactly 90 seconds of time.

Moment 2 — as a measure of energy

Second, a 'moment' is a measure of energy. The Moment Magnitude Scale (think an enhanced version of the old Richter scale) measures the actual size and magnitude of an earthquake the moment it strikes.

Moment 3 — as a unit of force

Third, a 'moment' is a unit of force. In physics, a 'moment' is the measure of how an object pivots or rotates around a specific point. For example, when you open a door and the door rotates around the hinges, this rotation is called a 'moment'.

MOMENT

=

A unit of time

A measure of energy

A unit of force

After exploring these three definitions and thinking about them a lot, I was very much taken with the word 'moment'. Just imagine how profoundly I could change my life if I combined these three 'moments' together to ensure I actually live in the moment and that I actually get shit done.

> # I could take just 90 seconds of time to generate enough energy to open a brand new door.

Combining the Moments to create MOMENTum

Adding the three moments together—that is, taking just 90 seconds of my time to use enough energy to open a brand new door in my life—was literally the only way I got myself into those skis and onto the ski lift and up to the top of that snow-covered mountain.

Without the simplicity of 'moments', skiing would not have happened—because the idea of skiing was simply too monumental. It was too audacious. It was too overwhelming. It was complex and complicated and how on earth was I supposed to get myself from Australia to France and onto a snow-covered mountain without any ski gear or experience or indeed any desire whatsoever to ski? I mean, come on.

On the other hand, exerting just 90 seconds of effort to open a new door is pretty simple.

Once you realise that goal setting, or approaching any new challenge or change in your life, requires just a 'moment'—then getting from point A to point B becomes elegantly doable.

In fact, everything becomes possible because you can do a hell of a lot in a 'moment'.

And once that new door is open, all you need to do is step through it. And then take another step and another and another because when you add one 'moment' to another 'moment' to another 'moment' and so on—you generate:

MOMENTum

the measurement of mass in motion

Holy shit.

I mean, the world 'moment' is actually in the word 'momentum'.

Momentum is the measurement of mass in motion. Simply put, any object that is moving has momentum. If you want to generate momentum, then *you* have to be moving. And how do you get moving? You take action. I didn't just decide one day in Melbourne, Australia, to go skiing for the first time in my life and then find myself in the French Alps the very next day decked out in a cute little ski suit, on skis, holding poles and shitting myself at the top of a run—I took action in the form of lots and lots of small steps towards that glorious, hairy goal and I self-generated a sense of momentum.

Thinking and acting small helped me knock off what was otherwise a very overwhelming goal that I thought was impossible to achieve.

And once you are in motion, it becomes very easy to stay in motion; you are on a roll.

Nothing is out of your reach. It will become, and continue to be, easier and easier to set outrageous goals and to implement them. Again and again. All by using the power of 'moments'.

Living my best life

And that's exactly how I truly started living my best life—a life by design. A life where I get to call all the shots on exactly what I want to do. And it is stupendous.

And isn't that what you want the rest of your life to be too? The best chapter yet? Where you routinely invest time in yourself to open new doors to create earth-shaking, life-changing experiences? A life where you are a little less selfless?

That's what this book is all about.

In Section I, I share with you my journey to mastering every moment to live an audacious life as a woman with no more (or much fewer) fucks to give. This section also covers the life-changing experiences that propelled me to create my first Life List. A Life List of everything I want to do while I am still young enough to enjoy doing them.

In Section II, I walk you through exactly how I created my Life List and show you how to design your own Life List—a perfect life from here on until forever.

In Section III, I share The Master Every Moment Framework: a step-by-step guide that shows you exactly how to implement and realise your magnificent Life List goals using the power of 'moments'.

And in Section IV, I share the very current iteration of my Life List, which I hope will inspire you in the creation and implementation of your own Life List.

By reading this book and creating your own Life List, you will get to live a big, spectacular, enormous, incredible, audacious life where you create, generate, experience and manifest a life that is:

MOMENTous

of great or lasting importance or consequence

And if that doesn't rock your world and knock your skis off then I don't know what will.

Section I

On Becoming Unapologetically Selfish (Or at Least a Little Less Selfless)

And so, I turned 50.

I have always loved my age, regardless of whatever it is at the time. I am not one of those people who frets about getting older. Most of the time I feel like I'm about 38 or 42, depending on the day.

But 50 is a milestone. It's a biggie. It's halfway to 100.

Approaching and then turning 50, along with everything else that was happening with my family around that point in time, did cause me to pause and to very intentionally challenge every single aspect of the life I was living.

I was 50 and my ex-husband was 54 and he was terminally ill. It was beyond confronting. What if I only had four years to live? Or months?

After Dan passed away I went through a period of time where every lump, twinge or general discomfort sent me into a genuine spiral of fear and a trip to the doctor. This fear wasn't so much for myself as for my children: if I too became terminally ill then my children would lose their mum as well as their dad. I projected this fear onto my own dad and every cough, sniffle or sneeze had me forcing him to go to the doctor too. *My kids have lost enough for now, thank you very much.*

After my personal and projected health crisis dissipated a little and I was less fearful for my imminent wellbeing, I spent a lot of my time in deep reflection about my life to date and what I want for the next part of my life. And here is what it comes down to for me.

I am a 50ish woman.

I have worked in some capacity—casual, part-time or fulltime— since I was 15 years old. I have worked as a lawyer in law firms and in the corporate world, I have worked as a senior executive in big business, and I have started my own businesses. I have always

---

(continued)

worked my arse off to be as magnificent as I can possibly be in every aspect of my life: daughter, sister, student, partner, parent, employee, employer, friend.

The day I turned 30 I gave birth to my first child. In quick succession I had two more pregnancies and had three young babies within three and a half years. I was the primary carer of my children and I continued to work and, with various iterations of success, downright failure and a good dose of grit and sheer survival, I managed to integrate motherhood with my career.

For much of the last 23 years of my life I have rarely prioritised myself—the order of my priorities has generally been my kids, my partner, my job, my parents and sisters, my friends, me. I have given and given and given some more.

For much of the last 23 years of my life, I have been the exact opposite of selfish. I have been monumentally selfless. I don't expect a prize for this. On the contrary, it makes me very much the same as literally every other woman I know—we are all quite fundamentally helpful, generous, altruistic givers.

My kids are now young adults and they are in the process of breaking up with me. It is a long, drawn out and often brutally painful break-up. Some days they want every part of me—mentally, emotionally and physically (having three incredibly noisy adult children play fight to sit on your lap for a cuddle in a competition to have you declare who you love the most is a very different experience to juggling three toddlers wanting to do the same), and then for days on end they simply aren't even here. They are at that stage in their own lives where they have one foot firmly planted in childhood and the other firmly planted in adulthood. And they get to choose which role they want to play on any given day: 'today I am a child and I need every ounce of you and can you please drop everything and book me a haircut because I don't like talking to strangers on the phone and can you also pay for it, Mum' OR 'today I am an adult and please get out of my way and don't let the door hit you on the arse, Mum'. I have spent 23 years being their primary carer, their biggest cheerleader, the love of their life—but I am being moved firmly across to the sidelines.

I am no longer the sun they need or want to orbit around.

All of which is normal and wonderful and right on time because my children are young adults and they are forging their own lives. But it's also heartbreaking. For me it feels like only yesterday that we were playing 'there were five in the bed and the little one said—roll over'.

However, it also means I have the opportunity to forge the next stage of my own magnificent life too. My children are no longer the sun that I need to orbit around.

I am only 53. I have my whole life ahead of me and I am desperate to live it stupendously. I feel like I have been waiting for this moment for years. I am very happily moving into the phase in my life where I get to experience the exquisite joy of becoming unapologetically selfish.

I am sick of working every hour god sent. And while I have always strived for and been fuelled by success in my career and business, I don't know exactly where the finish line is. I don't know when and where the previous part of the journey ends or what success in my future needs to look like. I don't know at what point in time I put the tools down, say that I have done and achieved enough and that it's now time to enjoy everything I have worked hard for.

My life to this point has been incredible and worthwhile and wonderful and exactly what it needed to be and I would not change a thing—but there's so much more to be had. Because I'm not sure whether all of this 'current state' I have been living is fulfilling enough for me any more.

I have ceaselessly compromised and I don't want to compromise any more.

I have ceaselessly nurtured my children and, while I will continue to love them endlessly, it is now time to nurture myself.

(continued)

I have ceaselessly made all of the decisions for everyone all of the time and I have had enough of decision making. It's not so much *decision fatigue* (my ability to make decisions is just fine) as *decision disinterest*. Sometimes I just want to hide away in a dark room so that the people looking for a decision to be made for them cannot find me.

I have money, my health, time and space. I have worked hard all my life and I am financially secure. I have worked hard on my self development to ensure that I am time affluent. I have worked hard to stay fit and healthy and energised.

I am tenacious. I am courageous. I am fearless. I am thriving professionally. I feel very good in my skin. I am brimming with wisdom and experience and knowledge. I am self-reliant and self-assured and somewhere along the journey my confidence and my common sense and my prudence and my self-knowledge have allowed me to discard that part of my ego that used to care what other people think of me. I am exactly where I need to be—which is, I am fast approaching a place of having no more fucks to give.

It is my turn.

And so these are the questions I have been pondering:

- I have spent so long climbing the ladder that all I can think right now is 'how the actual fuck do I get off?' And if and when I do get off, what am I going to do that fills the void? And how do I best give back the knowledge and experience and skills I have accumulated?

- What is next?

- How do I holistically change every aspect of my world so that I feel fulfilled in every part of my life?

- How do I start prioritising myself?

- And how do I find the women I need in my life who feel exactly the same way as I do so that we can work this out together?

I know I am not the only woman thinking deeply about her life. Every woman I know is having a challenging conversation with herself. Every woman I know has had an eventful journey to get to this point and none of those journeys have been effortless—we all have a backstory. It is your backstory that will help you shine the light on what you want your future-story to be. My backstory, particularly over the last five years, has been instrumental to how and why I now master every moment to live an audacious life.

Life is Too Short

After 22 years of marriage Dan left me.

Dan was a vital, charismatic man. He was the funniest person I ever met. He could light up a room. He was also supremely polarising—he was loved a lot or not at all. There were a lot of rules living with Dan.

And he loved me fiercely until he didn't. When he left, he told me that he wanted to fall in love again—with someone else—before it was too late.

I was angry. I was devastated. I was shocked. We had built a life together. We were part way through raising three amazing kids. We were a unit, a team, a partnership. We had planned our future and we were almost there, at the point where we could really start enjoying what we had achieved. And then it was gone. He was out. I felt like my future had been stolen from me.

Separating from your life partner is a brutal experience—regardless of who instigates the split. All of a sudden you are left wondering—who the hell is this person? How can you change so quickly from confidante, partner and co-pilot to stranger?

And then there is the fallout on the kids. Trying not to share with them or in front of them the tears and pain and anger and all of the wrongs and hurts and callous little incidentals that become so consuming.

And then there is negotiating a new way of being with your former partner. Our marriage was over—Dan wanted to be without me but he also wanted to be with me. He wanted to call me every day to tell me about his day. He wanted my advice. He wanted me to help him choose furniture. He wanted my friendship. Not because he wanted me back as his lover and partner, but because he wanted me back as his best friend. And that just wasn't part of the deal—you can't have all the good bits of a partnership and none of the bad bits. You can't walk away from the physical marriage but retain the emotional benefits.

And then there is the sheer publicity of separating. None of this plays out in private. Everyone gets a front row seat to the most traumatic event of your life. Everyone. We lived in a small suburb where everyone knows everyone else and their business—the kids were at school with or played sport with or travelled on the bus with or were friends with literally every other kid in town—and after we separated there seemed to be a community outpouring of grief and self-reflection.

'We thought you had the perfect marriage,' many said. 'What went wrong?'

What they were really saying was, *If this could happen to you, then it could happen to me. What did you do wrong, so that I can avoid doing the same thing?*

Or, 'You are so lucky he left you,' some said to me. 'My husband will never leave me and I can't afford to leave him.'

What they were really saying was, *I want to leave my marriage but I am too scared to walk away. I am frightened that I won't be able to support myself financially, and so I am stuck and I wish I was you because now you are free and your husband will feel so guilty at having left you that he will play fair with your financial settlement.*

I lost friends. Some people seemed to choose Dan. Others just stopped choosing me. Others still seemed worried that I might come and try to steal what belonged to them.

At the time all I could do was focus on my kids and myself. There was so much sadness and fear and loss and anger and confusion to work through.

I changed supermarkets. I shopped in sunglasses and headphones for months. I avoided the sad gazes. I tolerated the hugs.

During our marriage, Dan and I had travelled extensively. This didn't stop when we had our kids. We took them on some incredible adventures — we hiked the national parks and went to baseball games and Broadway shows in the United States; rode mountain bikes through the Dolomite Mountains in Italy; climbed Mount Etna; swam off boats in Greece, duck-diving for seashells; rode bikes through the Mekong Delta in Vietnam; and travelled Australia in caravans, fishing, swimming, surfing, canoeing, and living a life we loved. We created amazing memories.

After we separated, I prioritised my kids and I tried to normalise life for them as much as possible. I continued to travel with my kids, still creating memories.

But after we separated, Dan stopped doing this. For three and a half years after we separated, Dan didn't prioritise his children and he didn't prioritise shared experiences with them. He focused very much on his new life as a single man. He moved into a warehouse apartment that wasn't particularly kid friendly. He bought a large utility truck that wasn't particularly kid friendly. He didn't attend parent–teacher interviews, help with homework, make or attend doctor's appointments or insist on having the kids 50, 25, or even 10 per cent of the time. He just wasn't there.

Of course it was hard. Of course I would have welcomed the help and the emotional support. Of course it broke my heart that he was so self-absorbed that the kids were missing out on a relationship with their dad. But that was his choice and it was no longer my role to advise him, redirect him, or warn him of the damage he was doing to himself and his relationships.

And then Dan got sick and within 11 months he died and we lost him for a second time.

Sometimes the curveballs life throws at us are wrecking balls.

The usual expression is to 'battle' with cancer. In this case, there was no battle. The cancer was cunning. It arrived unannounced and spread its evil through Dan's body without fanfare. By the time he was aware that he was under attack it was too late. It was short and brutal and devastating. He was only 54. He left behind our three beautiful children to try to come to terms with a chasmal loss that they don't yet fully appreciate.

Life is too short.

That's another expression I used to offer up without appropriate respect. Before I would use it casually, dismissively, loosely. I would use it as a throwaway line to explain why I was doing something quite inconsequential.

After his diagnosis, Dan refocused on the kids and they spent a lot of time together in those last 11 months. Much of that time was really wonderful. Dan worked hard to keep his temper in check. But he had always been a 'my way or the highway' kind of guy and the kids, all late teens by then, were very well aware of what buttons to push and they pushed them repeatedly. Dan did his best to be better. And mostly he did and in the last months of his life he was a present and engaged and much-loved father.

In the final months of his life, when Dan still held out hope and his prognosis never seemed to be particularly definite, it felt to us all that Dan still had time. That it wasn't too late. And so he made plans. He found a deep-sea fishing tour to take the boys on in far north Australia. He found a luxury resort in Queensland to holiday with our daughter.

But he just deteriorated so quickly.

The three-to-four-day windows of time around chemotherapy that he needed for the trips slammed shut without notice. One day he was making plans and the next day his doctor said that he had a blood clot and that he could no longer fly. The fishing trip was out. The resort was out.

And so he found a house about a four-hour drive from where he lived and he booked it to stay with the kids for a few days. But again, too quickly, that window closed. He could no longer be too far away from the hospital just in case something went wrong.

Within weeks, days, his body began shutting down. It was so fast.

One of the many shitty things about cancer is that it doesn't come with a timeline. When you think you have time, suddenly you don't. But how much time do you have? It was so unclear.

Dan had decided that he wanted to die at home. On the Thursday he went into hospital for treatment and his doctors insisted he stay over the weekend. He was hopeful that he would be discharged on Monday to go home, but I knew that he wasn't going to leave the hospital this time. In retrospect I think the medical team knew that his death was fairly imminent and they wanted him to be comfortable.

My children were watching their father die before their eyes. They were grieving his loss before he had even gone and it was agony.

On the Monday he rang me in tears. He was scared and asked if I would come and see him. It was during COVID and there were rules and protocols and visiting hours and all of the bullshit associated with hospital visits. I think I made some sort of scene at reception, demanding entry. I remember playing the 'wife' card (which must have confused the hell out of them because he also had a girlfriend) and the 'my husband is dying' card and the 'he has rung me in tears' card.

He was so frightened. So small. So shrunken. I told him the sun was out and we were going for a walk. He didn't think this was allowed. 'Nonsense,' I said.

I asked for a wheelchair. I actually think I may have shrieked for one. The man I had loved for half my life, the father of my children, the man who could make me laugh harder than anyone else on earth, who I had travelled the world with, built a life with, created a partnership with, designed a future with—this vital, beautiful, charismatic man was days from death. It was beyond heartbreaking. Quite frankly I don't think anyone was prepared to challenge me over a wheelchair at this point in time.

We went for a walk around Fitzroy in Melbourne. We entered a flower shop and Dan ran his hands across the flowers, taking in all of their colours, and said how happy he was. How beautiful it all was. He lifted his head and closed his eyes and he basked in the sun. He must have been terrified.

I asked him if there was anything at all he wanted to do or wanted to see and he said that he wanted to drive to Point Lonsdale—where we had our family holiday home and had spent 18 years' worth of family holidays—with the kids. They would take the 75-minute trip down the freeway so they could look at the beach together. He wanted them to push him to the water in a wheelchair so he could put his feet in the waves.

But it was just too late.

After Dan passed away his executors told me that Dan wanted me to take our children on a family holiday. He wanted me to take the trip with them that he couldn't take. We were to go anywhere in the world and it was to be joyful and healing and incredible and celebratory. It was to represent the holidays he wished he had taken with his kids. It was to be the experience that he wished he'd prioritised when he was well. It was his gift to us to do what he ran out of time to do.

Because life is just too short.

It is too short to the point that we need to live it every single day. We need to think deeply about what is most important to us and we need to prioritise those things. We need to purposefully plan to invest our time for the greatest possible joy. We need to invest our time in the people we love most. We need to invest our time in creating memories, in being of service to others, in generating happiness and fulfilment and wonder. And we need to start doing this right now. Today. Because, quite frankly, to do otherwise is to risk being too late—and being too late is something we will regret forever.

Gaining Perspective and Gratitude

Grieving the death of your ex-husband is a complicated grief.

To start with, there is no real label for what I am. What do I even call myself in relation to Dan and losing him? I am the mother of his children and his ex-wife but I am not his widow, because even though we were not divorced, we were separated. After Dan's diagnosis and death, most people didn't really know how to engage or interact with me and my loss and so they carefully tiptoed around me. Mostly they asked after the kids and expressed a beautiful deep sympathy for their loss, but they didn't know how to comment on or touch on my loss, and so they didn't. They engaged with me purely as the mother of children who were grieving. And I completely understand this, because I had already lost Dan before.

But my loss and grief were and continue to be very deep. I grieve for losing him twice. I grieve for the years we don't have to co-parent and to rebuild our friendship. I miss him.

With the passing of time I have the capacity and the perspective to look at the end of my marriage and Dan's death through multiple lenses.

There is the lens where I realise that I didn't fight for our marriage. Not one little bit. I didn't ask Dan why he didn't want to fall back in love with me because I didn't want him to. I didn't suggest counselling. I didn't try and change his mind—not once. I was relieved it was over and that I could start my own life.

There is the lens where I realise that Dan and I just weren't in love with each other any more. And it was okay for him to want to feel really loved again, by someone else.

There is the lens where I realise we had wonderful times and awful times and now I really just prefer to remember all that was wonderful.

There is the lens where I know that I did all of the heavy lifting with our children during our marriage and after our separation. But that was a gift to me—because I got to spend all of my time with the most amazing people in the world. I have the memories, the love, the joy, the laughter, the pain, the scars and the angst. I have all of that and I treasure it.

There is the lens where I realise that after we separated we were solid at making parenting decisions together. We may not have always agreed with each other but we always presented a united front to the kids on the tough stuff. We told each other everything about the kids and all of the crazy, naughty, risk-taking lunacy they were getting up to, we agreed on an approach and then we backed each other up.

There is the lens where Dan told me how sorry he was for what he had done to our family by leaving our marriage. He was so very sorry too that he would not be there to help me help our kids deal with the grief of his death and the loss of their dad—'I'm leaving you with all the shit to clean up,' he said. Dan was also grieving his own death, he was of course acutely aware of what he was losing and the ramifications his death would have on us. He was devastated at the loss of everything he would no longer get to experience—like seeing his kids turn 21, walking his daughter down the aisle, standing alongside his sons when they married, holding his grandchildren, celebrating life with them. Right towards the end he dressed up in a tuxedo and he and our 17-year-old daughter recorded a father–daughter dance for her to play at her wedding. None of us has been able to watch it.

There is the lens where I grieve for my children's loss of their dad. Watching the pain and intense grieving they struggle with and knowing there is nothing I can do to take that pain away or to minimise their absolute devastation is a brutal and completely disempowering experience.

There is the lens where the lowest and most at loss I have ever felt also made me the strongest I have ever been.

There is the lens where I think about the women who projected onto me their fear that their husbands might choose a new love over their old love. I feel so desperately sad for them.

There is the lens where I think about the women who were envious that my husband had left me and they wished that their husband would leave them too. I feel so desperately sad for them.

And then there is the lens of knowing, really knowing in a visceral way, that putting things off until later might well be too late. Life is too short. It's too short to be sad, or mad, or angry, or lonely, or unfulfilled, or stagnant or resentful or bored.

With perspective comes growth and a determination to make changes in my life. After losing Dan for a second time I set about creating my Life List to ensure I live my best life.

And I want you to do exactly the same thing.

Don't put it off to do later. Because later might be too late.

Live Exactly How You Want

And what about you? What about your backstory?

You may not have kids, and boy oh boy have you been judged for that—each and every day. People often assume that you and the life you have lived to date are somehow *less than*. Really?

You may have kids and they are still young and/or dependent on you.

Or you may have older kids and they are in the process of breaking up with you right about now. You make eye-rolling jokes, don't adapt quickly enough to whatever is most politically correct today, and you spend most weekends hoping that pre-dinner drinks will be at someone else's house this time round. You are no longer cool and the best things about you are your credit card and your washing machine.

You might be an empty nester or about to be an empty nester or considering sneaking off into the night and assuming a new identity, which would in fact make your children empty nesters.

You may be single and would love to find new love.

You may be single and love your singledom.

You might be married or in a partnership and truly happily so.

You might be married or in a partnership and you are unhappy, or unfulfilled or sad or even lonely. And you are wondering whether this is the way you want to continue to live, and whether this is the person you want to live with, for the next 30 or so years of your life.

You might be separated or divorced or thinking about separating from your partner.

You might have lost your partner.

You might have parents who are increasingly relying on you to help them make the decisions that they previously made for you.

You may be feeling lonely.

You might be struggling to find like-minded women.

On any given day peri-menopause or full-blown menopause might be kicking your arse.

You are likely sagging in places you never thought it possible to sag.

When you need to complete an online form with your date of birth it's like spinning the wheel of fortune as you scroll down from this current year back into the last century.

You most certainly are a giver and a nurturer. You have spent a great deal of your life prioritising others over yourself.

You are tired.

Congratulations — you have officially reached what many like to dub your 'midlife'.

You are officially a woman of a 'certain age' and all of the associated labels that come with that.

Oh please. What a load of crap.

Personally I despise the term 'midlife'. Being 'our age' today is very different to when our mothers were 'our age' and worlds away from when our grandmothers were 'our age'. You are not old. You are not invisible. You are fit, youthful, energetic, sexy, sensual, confident, comfortable in your skin, thriving professionally, successful, full of life and champing at the bit to live life in a big and beautiful and spectacular way.

This is not a crisis — it is a catalyst.

You are a well-educated woman who suddenly has a little more time on your hands after growing and nurturing your vocation and/or a family for the last 20 to 30 years of your life.

You are cashed up and ready to spend. (*Forbes* gets you, describing women over 50 as 'super consumers' — 'with over $15 trillion in purchasing power [you] are the healthiest, wealthiest and most active generation in history'.)

You haven't changed, you just have the headspace right now to realise you want to do and be different.

And you will never be this young again, ever.

You may be thinking—'So, what happens next? Surely it's time to do things a little differently? To mix things up? To stop playing it so safe? To stop giving so much? To start doing the things I want to do while I am still young enough to enjoy them? To start being a little more selfish?'

You want more.

You want to invest in your future today.

You are moving into the phase in your life where you get to experience the exquisite joy of becoming unapologetically selfish.

Because life is too short. You only live once. And later might be too late.

Why Now?

When I personally reached the stage of having no more fucks to give—in the space of five years my husband left our marriage; I became a full time single mum to three teenagers; my mum passed away and left a gaping hole in all of our lives; I was terrified about not succeeding with my business; my ex-husband was diagnosed with cancer and passed away, and I was left to pick up all the pieces for my broken, grieving children, and the whole shit show was every bit as bad as you could possibly imagine—one thing that helped me get through those years was to take it moment by moment.

I know it sounds trite and like a sports coach encouraging the team to take it 'one game at a time', but it worked.

When I was in the absolute depths of grief accompanied by shock and loss and fear and uncertainty and confusion and exhaustion and I was grappling with saying and doing the right things every single day so as not to further break the fragile mental health of my children on top of my own relatively broken state of mind, taking things one day at a time was all I could do.

Because it was simply impossible for me to think beyond what each new day was going to serve up. We were bouncing from one trigger to the next and trying to think future or goals or tomorrow is just way too hard when you are just trying to survive today.

But that time has passed.

I am finally looking beyond today. I am no longer living day by day. I am no longer as needed by my kids. I finally have the energy, excitement, headspace and optimism to plan for my future.

And it's brilliant.

But it took a lot of work to get here. And at its heart, that is what this book is about:

- It's about sharing my story so that you know you aren't alone — that there are many women just like you who are reflecting on what's next.

- It's about inspiring you to seize control of your future, right now.

- It's about giving you proven frameworks to help you shortcut your journey from today to your magnificent future.

The first ever iteration of my Life List was partially prompted by the stark reminder of the fragility of life after Dan's diagnosis and death. But it was more than that. It was very much about having a pervasive feeling of general dissatisfaction with my life right now.

And the more women I speak to about this, the more I realise that we all seem to share this feeling of general unrest. Of general dissatisfaction.

Since writing and sharing my first Life List I have received so many messages of support from you—you have openly shared your stories about why now is exactly the right time for you too to take control, design your perfect life and write your own Life List. You are right on time.

The stories include partners who have lost their family's life savings; children diagnosed with terrible mental health conditions; separating from a life partner because you finally had the head space to realise you don't want another 30-plus years living the way you were living; realisations that being single is where you want to be; realisations that you love your life partner and have no intention of leaving your marriage but that you are also an individual who yearns to get more from your life than your partnership gives you; satisfaction that you are confident and incredible and wise and that your career is flourishing—and you want bigger and better and greater experiences; or dissatisfaction with your current career and a deep desire to reinvent yourself.

Because one thing is for sure—it's your turn now. Let's make this spectacular.

Take a few moments to reflect and answer these questions:

Why are you here?

Why do you want to create your Life List?

Why now?

Before My Life List Was Even a Life List

In 2019 my 15-year-old daughter was on a five-month student exchange from Australia to France. She was desperately unhappy, did not love her hosts who appeared to have a very sink or swim approach to assimilating a non-French-speaking teen into life on the other side of the world, and spent many nights (at 2 am my time) on the phone to me in tears.

As she counted down the months to when she could return home, I decided to fly to France as a surprise and to extricate her from the depths of her despair two weeks earlier than the scheduled end of her exchange. With visions of the two of us traipsing around Paris Audrey Hepburn–style, I booked my plane ticket.

A few weeks out from my departure on one particularly agony-filled phone call, and in order to cheer my daughter up, I told her that I was coming to her rescue—we would spend two weeks in Paris in a little apartment, eating baguettes and cheese, shopping and visiting the sites and she would speak French and it would be wonderful.

And while she was thrilled that I was coming over, she clearly had other ideas: 'Mum, can we go skiing?'

Huh?

Skiing? Really? What about Paris, honey?...Honey?

Every fibre of my body was opposed to the idea of skiing. I was about to turn 50, had never skied in my life, and having spent the best part of my

49 years living in Australia and spending all of my holidays somewhere warm, I literally shuddered at the thought of being cold and wet and with snow in my undies. I mean, come on.

But I pushed through and I made it happen.

Within a month of our return from that trip, Dan was diagnosed with cancer and within 11 months of his diagnosis he had died. And my whole approach to my life changed.

I wanted to do more, be more, and live more.

My two goal-setting epiphanies

I have always been goal driven—I have been raising that bar higher and higher for myself ever since I could jump.

As a time management specialist I am very fond of processes and frameworks—a great framework will save a lot of time and will guarantee the right results every single time.

So, I set about pulling apart and seriously examining the exact steps I had taken to get myself from the beach in Melbourne to the top of that snow-covered mountain in France in the face of great self-resistance. And it struck me that in my quest to do more and be more and live more, I had been doing goal setting very wrong up until now in two big ways.

First, I had always set and tackled my goals one at a time (e.g., I want to go to university to study Law—done; I want to buy my first car—done; I want to travel the world before I start working—done; I want to be a mum—done; I want to work part-time—done; I want to start my own business—done, etc.). This had always served me well and I had steadily achieved a lot of what I had set out to achieve in my life.

However, from now on if I was to live the big, audacious life by design that I was in the process of envisioning, then tackling my goals one at a time would no longer cut it. In order to live stupendously I needed a huge, grand, brilliant, all-encompassing plan for what I wanted my life to look like over the next year, five years, and 10 years plus. I call this plan my Life List.

Second, if I was to have this all-encompassing plan—my Life List—as opposed to continuing to tackle life one goal at a time, then I needed to be much more considered about how I approached the execution of my goals. It wasn't enough just to have the Life List; I also needed a framework to make that Life List happen.

What I did with my epiphanies

My two goal-setting epiphanies meant I needed two distinct frameworks, a *designing* stage and a *doing* stage, and I needed to make sure they worked together seamlessly.

The *Designing* stage: my Life List is the tapestry of the life I want to live. In undertaking the design stage, I created a long, long list of everything I want to do in my life while I am still young enough to enjoy it. To help you design your own Life List I created The Life List Framework. You can read about and follow The Life List Framework in Section II of this book. I also created a beautiful Life List Planner for you to use to design your own Life List (go to www.katechristie.com.au to download your Life List Planner for free).

The *Doing* stage: it isn't enough to just design a Life List—it looks pretty on paper and it sounds amazing and wouldn't that just be wonderful—but without action, ultimately it is just a list. My second framework—The Master Every Moment Framework—ensures you will turn up and actually implement your Life List goals. You can read about and follow The Master Every Moment Framework in Section III. The Life List

Planner provides the template for you to implement every step of The Master Every Moment Framework.

I am now living my best life as designed in my Life List by actively and systematically following the steps in The Master Every Moment Framework. A key Go Big Goal (you can read more about these in Section II of this book) on my Life List is to help as many other women as possible live their best life too, which is what this book is all about.

A life by design.

Section II

The Life List Framework

Your Life List is an ever-changing collection of your goals, dreams, passions and aspirations. It is a single place where you can actively record all of the things you want to achieve or experience in your life while you are still young enough to fully achieve, experience and enjoy them. It is a place where you can record your progress, write your reflections, express your gratitude for your amazing life, contemplate your growth and keep yourself accountable. It is a testimony of the awesome next chapter you are about to enter.

Five months after Dan died I sat down and wrote my first comprehensive Life List — as part of my healing but also because of my determination to live the rest of my life very differently. Gone was any sense of complacency or idleness — it was time for action. It was time to play a much bigger role in designing my future.

My first Life List was published in *CEOWORLD Magazine* in September 2021. That first iteration of my Life List is extracted below and it continues to provide inspiration to me every day.

Life is too short — so I'm going to:

- Love my kids every single minute
- Swim every day
- Stand up for myself
- Eat lollies (not donuts)
- Set and smash audacious goals
- Do one incredible 'first' for me every year
- Focus on the right things at the right time
- Get 10 hours of sleep every night
- Have a weekly massage
- Exercise daily

(continued)

- Stay out of email
- Say No when I might otherwise have said Yes
- Say Yes when I might otherwise have said No
- Charge what I'm worth
- Stop spending money on stuff I don't need
- Declutter, simplify and streamline
- Stop caring who will take the bins out
- Unplug
- Stop investing my precious time on the wrong tasks
- Stop investing my precious time on the wrong people
- Reject being complacent
- Embrace being courageous
- Focus on what makes me happy
- Stop sweating the small stuff
- Stop sweating some of the big stuff
- Ensure I don't tread water waiting for something better to come along
- Forgo vacuuming
- Focus on my mental health
- Spend winter in the sun because I don't like being cold
- Be grateful
- Be curious
- Hang with my kids exactly when they want to hang
- Value my values
- Work less and less and play more and more
- Get rid of the clothes I never wear

- Spend a lot of time with my dad

- Honour my posse of awesome women

- Climb mountains

- Buy an amazing apartment in the city which has two bedrooms which then semi-forces my kids to move out and start living their best lives (in their own houses)

- Tell my kids that I love them every single day even when they are shitting me

- Never hold grudges

- Check for lumps

- Read every day

- Travel

- Let go of possessions that no longer bring me joy

- Cuddle and kiss my kids every chance I get

- Stop feeling guilty for choosing takeaway over cooking

- De-vest in toxic people

- Spend time with my beautiful sisters

- Lie under the doona all day watching movies when the mood strikes

- Swear

- Stop living my second best life and start living my best life

- Help other people design and live their best lives

My Life List has continued to evolve as I evolve. I have already implemented, completed or am actively living some of the goals from my original Life List. (Section IV of this book includes the current iteration of my Life List.)

In this section, I share The Life List Framework and you will design your own magnificent Life List — the tapestry of the life you want to live.

The Life List Framework has three steps: you will establish your Life List Rules for what goals make the cut onto your Life List; you will learn about and include goals across the 7 Life List Chapters; and you will learn about the three different types of goals you need to experience.

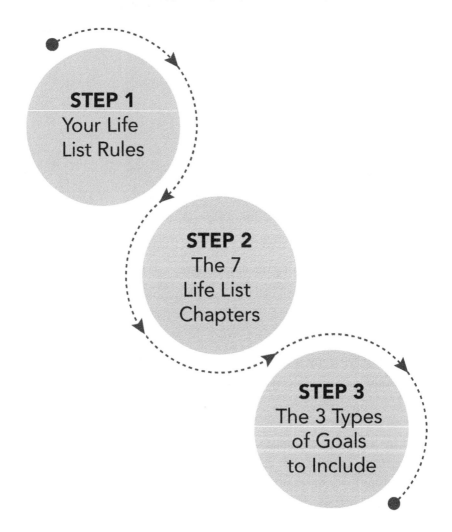

STEP 1
Your Life
List Rules

STEP 2
The 7
Life List
Chapters

STEP 3
The 3 Types
of Goals
to Include

But First, Some Goal-Setting Basics

There are many resources you can tap into to help you set your goals. It can take hours of research just to find your way through this stuff. Who has the time? Me — happily, I took a bullet for you on this one.

Ultimately, after reading as much as I could on goal setting and goal smashing, I created my own frameworks for how to successfully *design* and then *do* my Life List. That's kind of the ultimate end game isn't it? Find something that works for you and stick to it. And if you can't find something that works for you, then make it up for yourself (and stick to it).

I have tested The Life List Framework and The Master Every Moment Framework on thousands of my clients and audience members to make sure that they work — and they do. I have refined and tweaked the frameworks to make them as simple, doable, and achievable as possible. With the help of your ongoing feedback and insights I will continue to refine the frameworks so that we can all succeed together in designing and living out our best lives.

Before we jump into The Life List Framework, it's good to understand some goal-setting basics:

1. *Pick up a pen.* The act of writing your goals down — on paper — will significantly increase your chances of achieving them. Thinking about or visualising or even typing out your goals isn't quite enough. Multiple studies support this thinking — and if it's an area that interests you, I encourage you to explore the neuroscience and research that underpin successful goal setting.

But in a nutshell, the benefits I personally like the most about the physical act of writing down my goals on paper—especially in my Life List—are that:

» in order to articulate a goal in writing I first need to visualise exactly what it is I want to achieve, and this creates a picture in my mind that I can draw on when I need it, creating a strong emotional connection with the outcomes I want to achieve

» the act of writing enhances my ability to recall the goal

» the act of writing gives me clarity and focus, which in turn generates enormous excitement and motivation

» the act of getting my thoughts out of my head and onto paper frees up space in my brain for more thinking.

So get your pen out, lady.

2. *Control works.* Research shows that when we feel in control of our lives we are more likely to be psychologically and physically healthy. Creating a Life List is a process of joy—but it is also intended to give you a strong sense of control over your own destiny. Be aware that by setting goals you are engaging in an act of control—this is literally a life by design.

3. *Be specific.* Your goals need to be very concrete. This can be challenging when it comes to setting the Go Big Goals that have a lot of moving parts. Breaking bigger goals into smaller, bite-sized steps or actions that are all specific and concrete will significantly increase your chances of succeeding with the goal. Each of these smaller steps or actions must have a deadline and be measurable—and it can also help to celebrate achieving them.

4. *Sharing creates momentum.* Studies suggest that working collaboratively and sharing your goals and your progress towards achieving them with a friend or cohort of supporters can help you stay on track. For this reason I have set up a closed Facebook group for us so that we have a private group of like-minded, supportive, awesome women that we can share and celebrate our Life List with. Instructions for how to apply to join the Facebook group can be found on my website at www.katechristie.com.au.

Let's jump into The Life List Framework.

STEP 1
Your Life
List Rules

STEP 2
The 7
Life List
Chapters

STEP 3
The 3 Types
of Goals
to Include

When designing your Life List you need to know what makes a goal impactful and important enough to be included in your Life List.

Bottom line, none of us is looking to live a bland life here. You wouldn't be reading this book if you were set on a vanilla future.

In order to decide what makes the cut, reflect on *why* any given goal is one you want to add to your Life List. Sometimes it will be for the sheer fun of it, or because it is a completely new experience, or because deep down it is something that you have always wanted to experience, or because it will make the world a much better place.

> To keep you focused on your *why,* there is room in The Life List Planner under each separate goal to include your 'Reflection' on why the goal is important to you.

Next, and to ensure that your Life List contains a full kaleidoscope of colours and flavours as well as some incredible stretch goals (as opposed to a list of experiences that you would probably have gotten around to doing anyway at some stage), it's important to set yourself a few rules as to what makes the cut.

My personal Life List Rules help me decide what is impactful enough to be included in my Life List. In order to be included, for me, a goal must be at least one (and preferably more than one) of the following:

1. *Glorious.* It must be joyful, exciting, purely audacious or give me the warm glow of having achieved something truly spectacular.

2. *Challenging.* It must challenge me physically, mentally, emotionally or spiritually.

3. *Outside my comfort zone.* It must have the squirm factor — this is different to being 'challenging' because some goals that I might find challenging (such as climbing a big mountain) don't make me squirm at the thought of doing them (such as going speed dating).

4. *New.* It must be something I have never experienced before.

This is how I want to live the rest of my life. Anything and everything is up for grabs.

Think about your own Life List Rules — what will it take for a goal to make it onto your Life List? You might decide to adopt my rules for your own Life List, or make up your own.

Before I die I want to ... Stop! This isn't a bucket list

A bucket list is generally defined as a list of the things you would like to experience before you die — that is, before you 'kick the bucket'.

This is not a bucket list.

There are a few things that I don't like about the concept of a 'bucket list', which is why we are creating a Life List. Bucket lists:

- often focus almost exclusively on travel and adventure. What about everything else that's important to you living a many-faceted brilliant life, such as giving and learning and growth and curiosity and joy and health and wellbeing?

- often focus on crazy travel and adventure experiences such as swimming with sharks dressed in a wetsuit looking like a very edible seal, or jumping out of a tiny plane with a piece of silk attached to your back by a string, or throwing yourself off a bridge with a rubber band tied around your ankles — scary shit that may hasten your actual kicking of the bucket.

- are often actively implemented only later in life. The World Tourism Organisation in their 'Tourism 2020' forecast projects that by 2050, more than 2 billion international tourists will be aged 60 and older (up from 593 million in 1999). Sadly, these 'older' travellers will be required to pay a premium on travel insurance because the research relied on by insurance companies when they set their premiums shows that the over 60s are at higher risk of travel-associated morbidity and mortality. Travel insurance becomes a lot more expensive for people over 65, can double from the age of 70 and can even become unavailable for those over 75.

- can look and feel a bit like a list of obligations — the things you never, ever made time for in your life but which now you need to get through lickety-split and tick them off the bloody list before you die ... from exhaustion.

- are often prompted by a near-death experience such as a personal poor health prognosis. And then there is a scramble to experience all the things you have been putting off until later because suddenly it is later. Certainly losing Dan at such a young age was the catalyst for me to start thinking about the fragility of life — but I am hell-bent on living it to the full right now. Because why wait to start living?

And so our list is not a bucket list. Our list is a Life List. It's all about identifying the amazing things we want to experience across every facet of our lives while we are still young enough to enjoy them.

Don't ask: what do I want to do before I die?

Ask:
what do I want
to do while I'm
still young enough
to enjoy it?

STEP 1
Your Life
List Rules

STEP 2
The 7
Life List
Chapters

STEP 3
The 3 Types
of Goals
to Include

Your Life List is not intended to just be about creating fun experiences and adventures or a wish list of destinations you want to travel to. It is so much more than that. It needs to be made up of the many fundamentals of your life that are most important to you and it must include the habits you want to form and the behaviours you are no longer prepared to tolerate (in yourself or in others).

STEP 2
The 7 Life List Chapters

I think of all of these elements as chapters of the book of my life, and so I have broken these fundamentals into 7 Life List Chapters.

For each of the 7 Life List Chapters you need to include goals that are just for you and also those goals that you want to experience with, or have an impact on, your family, the community you live in, and the world.

It's important to have goals in your Life List that meet individual chapters from the 7 Life List Chapters (for example, getting my finances under control sits very firmly in the Wealth Chapter). But equally, I like to curate goals that cut across multiple Life List Chapters (for example, hiking 130 km of the Larapinta Trail hit the Health & Wellbeing Chapter, the Adventure Chapter, and the Lifestyle & Environment Chapter). Goals that touch on multiple chapters feel more all-encompassing and, to be honest—even more stupendous.

The 7 Life List Chapters are:

1. *The Health & Wellbeing Chapter* includes everything you want to do and experience to maximise your physical, emotional, mental and spiritual health and wellbeing, including exercise, diet, meditation, rest, healing, acceptance and forgiveness.

2. *The Wealth Chapter* includes everything you want to do to ensure you grow your financial security, including savings, wealth creation, investments, superannuation and estate planning.

3. *The Adventure Chapter* includes all of the experiences, travel and adventures that will make your soul sing.

4. *The Growth Chapter* includes learning, curiosity, the pursuit of knowledge and spectacular career goals.

5. *The Giving Chapter* includes all of the pursuits and opportunities you want to create where you generously give or contribute your time, knowledge or money.

6. *The Relationships Chapter* includes the relationships you want to create, nourish or grow and those you want to change or let go.

7. *The Lifestyle & Environment Chapter* includes how, where and the way you want to live your life and how you want to influence or contribute to the environment around you, the habits you want to adopt or change and the behaviours you want to let go.

In identifying your goals, dreams and aspirations for your Life List and filling the 7 Life List Chapters, ask yourself the following types of questions:

- What have I always wanted to do but haven't because *(insert your reason of choice: e.g. I let the needs of others come first; I let the demands of others come first; I wasn't allowed to do it; I didn't have the time/money/motivation/strength/ resources/energy)*?

- What will bring me joy?

- What will give me a sense of wonder?

- Where have I always wanted to go?

- What will give me a sense of deep satisfaction, achievement or pride?

- How can I best contribute to the happiness, knowledge, wellbeing, joy or quality of life of others?

- What do I want to learn?

- What will I regret not doing?

- What do I really want to challenge myself to do or be?

- What do I want my legacy to be?

- What do I want to change?

- What do I want to let go of?

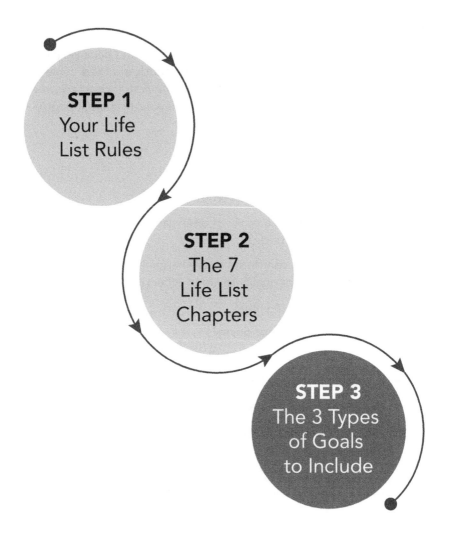

STEP 1
Your Life
List Rules

STEP 2
The 7
Life List
Chapters

STEP 3
The 3 Types
of Goals
to Include

There are three different types of goals you need to include in your Life List:

1. Go Big Goals

2. Go Small Goals

3. Go Now Goals.

Go Big Goals

Your Life List absolutely must include a broad range of magnificent, big, audacious, utterly outrageous, awesome, life-changing goals. These goals should cut across the 7 Life List Chapters, or multiple chapters at once, so that you are actively fulfilling all of the most important parts of your life.

The bigger the goal the more planning, sequencing, vision boarding and dreaming you will need to do, including breaking the Go Big Goals down into smaller steps or actions that you can implement over the coming months and years. (More on this in Section III under The Master Every Moment Framework.)

For the first few years of my Life List I set myself the challenge to live out one Go Big Goal every year—for example:

- in year 1 it was swimming in the sea every day for a full year
- in year 2 it was walking the Larapinta Trail in central Australia.

On completing the Larapinta, which hit all four of my Life List Rules big time, I realised that the whole Go Big Goal thing is pretty damn

(continued)

> addictive. And so I now actively engage in completing a number of Go Big Goals a year.
>
> You can follow and stay current with my Life List on my website where I actively share what I am planning for next, along with what I have just completed—at www.katechristie.com.au.

You might want to engage in one Go Big Goal a year or you might be at the stage in your life where you want to engage in a Go Big Goal more regularly.

The key is to have a Life List that you actively engage in.

Go Small Goals

Your Life List should also include a range of smaller, life-affirming, inspiring goals that provide the daily fuel that makes your soul sing.

Go Small or short-term goals can be implemented in the near future and generally without extensive planning.

Be careful not to overload your list with these goals—while it's good to have Go Small Goals in your Life List, you don't want so many small goals that your Life List starts to feel more like a shopping list that you quickly work through so that you can be home on the couch in front of the TV by 7 pm.

Go Now Goals

Be spontaneous! Be brave! Take a chance! Just say yes!

What's the worst thing that can happen? (Actually, if it involves making the front page of the newspaper tomorrow then maybe pull back a little ...)

Keep space on your Life List Planner to backfill after you do something that is spontaneous and simply awesome. Where you think — *OMG, that wasn't even on my Life List but it so should have been, I just didn't think of it at the time, but if I had thought of it, it would have been there to start with, so ... yeah ... god I am awesome.*

Then come back and update your Life List Planner so you have a complete record of the fact that you are absolutely killing it.

What not to include

Keep your Life List free of anything that:

- feels like an obligation

- does not make your heart sing

- is really just someone else's expectation of what you should be doing with your life.

This is your Life List, not your Family's Life List or your Partnership Life List (both of which I very much encourage you to design at some stage — just not right now because this is *all about you*). Having said that, there will be Life List items that involve bringing joy to others — your family, friends, the charities you volunteer for, the community — so don't be afraid to add them in (provided they meet at least one of your Life List Rules).

It's time to write your own Life List

You can find The Life List Planner at www.katechristie.com.au—it is a free resource that you are welcome to print out and it's designed to help you with your own Life List journey.

Light a candle, play your favourite music and get creative.

Drafting your own Life List can be done in one luxurious session of self-reflection or over the course of many days. It should be updated again and again so that it remains current—because it needs to expand as your fresh outlook on this next part of your life expands.

You can create your Life List in multiple drafts—treat your first iteration as a laundry list of everything that comes to mind and write it all down as the inspiration strikes you.

Be conscious of including goals that cover all 7 Life List Chapters (see Step 2).

Include both Go Big Goals and Go Small Goals (see Step 3). There is also space in your Life List Planner to come back later to include any acts of spontaneity—Go Now Goals—that you want a record of and want to reflect on (see Step 3).

Work through the first draft of your goals and delete anything that doesn't feel quite right, or right for now, so that you have an extensive list of what is most important to you for your future.

If you like your Life List to look neat and tidy and pretty then write it up again (I admit that I am that girl who loves to write up my Life List with a special pen, loads of colours and little doodles and using my best handwriting).

Send me an email telling me how you are going with your Life List. Let me know what goals you have completed and how you are feeling—I would love to hear about your Life List and I will be there to cheer you on—email me at kc@katechristie.com.au.

Bring It All to Life

I hear you. It's all very well and good to have a beautiful, colourful Life List that looks oh so pretty as it sits on your desk under a fine film of dust — but just how on earth do you turn your Life List into a reality?

On any given day, especially when I first started working on my Life List, I could come up with a thousand reasons as to why today was just not the day to get my arse into gear. You can read more about this enormous long list of reasons (a.k.a. excuses), along with how to overcome them, in Section III — The Master Every Moment Framework. And I am prepared to bet money that you will recognise many of these excuses, as they will most likely be the exact same ones you roll out each time you are faced with a goal or an opportunity that feels too hard to chase down.

I promise you that those days are over.

I overcame my stagnation and my uncertainty and my hesitation, along with that long list of excuses, a long time ago. I simply bloody love my life.

And don't you want that too?

Let me hear a HELL YES!

Good. Because you can have exactly what I have.

You can live out your own Life List with exactly the same level of enjoyment, courage, enthusiasm and joy that I live out mine.

That long list of excuses no longer applies to me. I have changed my mindset and have flexed my goal-setting/goal-smashing muscles so often that I have created an incredibly powerful muscle memory that works for me every single time. I simply cannot fail at goal setting and goal smashing.

How did I do it?

I created The Master Every Moment Framework and it ensures I get shit done.

Congratulations! You have created your stunning Life List!

Send me an email and share your Life List with me and let me know how you feel: kc@katechristie.com.au

Section III

The Master Every Moment Framework

Your Life List—which you have now prepared using your Life List Planner, and which is sitting in front of you like a shiny new toy ready for you to play with—is the *design* part of the process.

The Master Every Moment Framework is the *doing* part of the process, and it is critical.

Like any trusted and true framework, I built The Master Every Moment Framework retrospectively off the back of successfully achieving what—at that point in time in my life—was the hardest physical and mental challenge I had ever experienced: skiing for the first time.

Skiing—which from here on I will refer to as the 'Great Ski Adventure'—literally tested my resolution in every way imaginable. But I did it, I went skiing. It may not have been entirely pretty at the time, but I knew that my success in achieving this (otherwise impossible) goal meant that there must be a successful process in there somewhere. And, if I could extract the nuggets that made up that success, I could perfect a process that would become a replicable framework to help me achieve all of my goals in the future.

Ultimately, it was a combination of a multitude of steps, and not just two or three key actions, that helped me achieve the momentous experience of the Great Ski Adventure. And so, I examined in detail and pulled apart every single step I took to get my bum off the beach and onto the ski slopes—and I created The Master Every Moment Framework. The framework works for me, it works for my clients and it will work for you.

The Master Every Moment Framework is essentially a map that is structured to ensure you tap into and power up your self-discipline skill set: it will jump-start your ability to get moving with your goals, drive you to persevere when the going gets a little tough, and keep you motivated and focused on the outcomes you want to achieve. The Master Every Moment Framework makes it supremely easy for you to action and celebrate your

Life List. Work through it at your own pace, enjoy every second and make sure you keep me posted on your progress.

The Master Every Moment Framework is broken into three parts:

Part 1: MOMENT has five planning steps to help you lay the foundation on which you are going to build your magnificent goals. Part 1: MOMENT will get you moving.

Once you are moving, Part 2: MOMENTum has five steps designed to keep you moving and to ensure you set yourself up for absolute success. This part is action driven—you will be actively working towards the attainment of your goals, and each of the five steps helps build a massive sense of momentum (of course!) and excitement. Seriously, nothing can stop you now.

Part 3: MOMENTous is the execution stage of The Master Every Moment Framework—where you get to experience the goal, celebrate your success along with the journey, and then reflect on what you have learned, experienced and what you are grateful for.

The Master Every Moment Framework is the roadmap that I want you to use every time you select a goal to conquer from your Life List.

We are going to work through The Master Every Moment Framework together and you will see exactly how smashing the Great Ski Adventure goal gave me the steps that would ultimately become The Master Every Moment Framework.

I have also set out the Great Ski Adventure as a fully worked up goal at the back of my Life List Planner so you can see how to work up your own goals.

The Master Every Moment
Framework

MOMENT

1. Set Your Intention
2. Pick a Goal
3. Identify Your Resisting Forces
4. Identify What You Most Value
5. Lock in a Deadline for the Goal

1. Mind Map the Goal
2. Lock in Deadlines for Each Action
3. Find Your Cheer Squad
4. Reframe Your Goal
5. Take a Step

MOMENTum

MOMENTous

1. Do It!
2. Celebrate
3. Share with the Squad
4. Acknowledge Your Growth and Lessons
5. Express Your Gratitude

Take 90 seconds to generate enough energy to open a new door

It's time to give
yourself the gift of
a Moment.

MOMENT

1. Set Your Intention
2. Pick a Goal
3. Identify Your Resisting Forces
4. Identify What You Most Value
5. Lock in a Deadline for the Goal

1. Mind Map the Goal
2. Lock in Deadlines for Each Action
3. Find Your Cheer Squad
4. Reframe Your Goal
5. Take a Step

MOMENTum

MOMENTous

1. Do It!
2. Celebrate
3. Share with the Squad
4. Acknowledge Your Growth and Lessons
5. Express Your Gratitude

MOMENT

In Part 1: MOMENT, we will combine the three definitions of the word 'Moment' to exert just 90 seconds of energy to open a brand new door in your life. Part 1 is deliberately the only part of The Master Every Moment Framework that is time bound—because we all have 90 seconds we can spare. It's a super quick injection of motivation.

Use these 90 seconds to get you in the goal-smashing mood—you will focus on your genuine intention to live a wonderful, big, magnificent, audacious life, select the next goal you want to conquer, identify what might get in your way and what will help you push through regardless, and set a deadline for when you will complete your goal.

Part 1: MOMENT is a 90-second pre-planning masterclass designed to get you moving. There are 5 steps which are designed to ensure you lay the foundation on which you are going to build your audacious life. It's thrilling!

MOMENT

1. **Set Your Intention**
2. Pick a Goal
3. Identify Your Resisting Forces
4. Identify What You Most Value
5. Lock in a Deadline for the Goal

1. Mind Map the Goal
2. Lock in Deadlines for Each Action
3. Find Your Cheer Squad
4. Reframe Your Goal
5. Take a Step

MOMENTum

MOMENTous

1. Do It!
2. Celebrate
3. Share with the Squad
4. Acknowledge Your Growth and Lessons
5. Express Your Gratitude

1 Set Your Intention

In 1687 Isaac Newton published his three laws of motion. Newton's First Law of Motion, also known as the law of inertia, states that 'an object at rest stays at rest'. If you are not moving, you are not moving. Simple. I call Newton's first law the law of 'What's on Netflix?'

Happily, however, the reverse is also true—while an object at rest stays at rest, an object in motion stays in motion.

It's time to shake off your inertia and get moving. It's time to decide to open a new door—because that is where the magic happens.

In **Step 1: Set Your Intention**, take **10 seconds** to frame your mind to embrace a life by design. I want you to generate a simple yet powerful intention to implement and live out your Life List and ensure that you live stupendously from here on out.

Your intention might be something like:

- *I am [age], cashed up and with no more fucks to give.*

- *I want this. It's my turn.*

- *It's time to live stupendously.*

- *This is my life and I get to design it. I am fully committed to doing this for me.*

- *I'm excited that my kids are now independent. I have time and money and opportunities. I want this next chapter to be called 'Me' and it will be the best chapter of all.*

- *I have worked hard forever and now it's time to reframe exactly how I want to live.*

Or come up with your own beautifully crafted intention that brings you a sense of optimism, infinite opportunity and focus.

Once you become addicted to implementing your Life List goals using The Master Every Moment Framework you might not need to complete this step each and every time you set about implementing a new goal. But for the first few Go Big Goals you chase after, it is very useful to focus on your intention to live a life by design. Plus, if at any stage you take a break from goal setting and smashing, then when you return to implementing your Life List you should make sure you include intention setting.

My Great Ski Adventure

My intention

It's time to switch things up. Be Bold!

Well done. You are 10 seconds into your first MOMENT.

1. Set Your Intention
2. **Pick a Goal**
3. Identify Your Resisting Forces
4. Identify What You Most Value
5. Lock in a Deadline for the Goal

1. Mind Map the Goal
2. Lock in Deadlines for Each Action
3. Find Your Cheer Squad
4. Reframe Your Goal
5. Step + Step + Step

MOMENTum

1. Do It!
2. Celebrate
3. Share with the Squad
4. Acknowledge Your Growth and Lessons
5. Express Your Gratitude

2 Pick a Goal

In **Step 2: Pick a Goal,** take **10 seconds** to pick one goal from your Life List.

I encourage you to choose a Go Big Goal—be outrageous, be audacious. That's what you are here for. Think about those goals where your reflection as to why you chose the goal (reflections are covered in Step 2 of The Life List Framework) feels most impactful to you. Importantly, choosing a Go Big Goal will also give you the opportunity to work through a huge goal using The Master Every Moment Framework with my support.

Think about your Life List Rules and choose something you have never done before—that thing you know you will one day regret not having done while you were still young enough to enjoy it.

Or choose something that you have done before and which you somehow lost sight of and want to reintroduce into your life because it is meaningful to you.

Or choose something that will make you super proud of yourself.

Or choose something so momentous that just thinking about it puts a smile on your face.

For mine, I had never been skiing before. I gave myself 10 seconds to decide to be audacious—10 seconds to say 'YES—I'm going to go skiing in France with my daughter.'

My Great Ski Adventure

MY Go Big Goal: Skiing in France

Well done. You are 20 seconds into your first MOMENT.

1. Set Your Intention
2. Pick a Goal
3. **Identify Your Resisting Forces**
4. Identify What You Most Value
5. Lock in a Deadline for the Goal

1. Mind Map the Goal
2. Lock in Deadlines for Each Action
3. Find Your Cheer Squad
4. Reframe Your Goal
5. Take a Step

MOMENTum

1. Do It!
2. Celebrate
3. Share with the Squad
4. Acknowledge Your Growth and Lessons
5. Express Your Gratitude

3

Identify Your Resisting Forces

In **Step 3: Identify Your Resisting Forces** I want you to take **30 seconds** to identify your personal resisting forces—exactly what is going to stop you in your tracks and upend your chosen Go Big Goal before you even get to the starting gates?

Often the incredible, magnificent, audacious goals we set for ourselves—those amazing opportunities we flirt with, the big dreams we dream, or the extraordinary ideas we come up with (or which others come up with for us, such as skiing)—begin as an exciting spark of inspiration that provides an immediate rush of adrenalin.

What an amazing idea!

But then the very next emotion we feel is one of resistance. Reality bites and we put that big idea, dream or goal on permanent hold because it is just too big, too hard, too cold, too wet, too dangerous, too not me, too expensive, too much, too ...

Sir Isaac Newton's Second Law of Motion states that 'the rate of change of momentum in an object is directly proportional to the force applied to it'. This second law explains exactly why it is so difficult to jump at that audacious goal—because your brain is fighting against all of your pre-conditioned behaviours and old habits (or forces) that may be greater and stronger and supremely resistant to the force you are trying to generate to move forward.

You have identified (in Step 2: Pick a Goal) the goal you want to work on. But straight away your pesky little brain kicks into gear to talk you out of that magnificent idea by telling you exactly why you can't do it. Worse still, there might be people around you who get in your ear to tell you exactly why you can't do it (more on this later).

This was certainly the case with the Great Ski Adventure. After an initial adrenalin rush and perhaps 10 seconds imagining how goddamn cute

I would look as a ski bunny in France, carving up the snow and being spotted by a talent scout for a 50ish women's ski brand who signs me up on the spot to be their brand ambassador and ... the doubts and fears rudely intruded.

Skiing?! Are you shitting me?

And just like that — within seconds — I wrote off the whole Great Ski Adventure.

It was too hard. It was too expensive. I don't like being cold. Or wet. Or broken. Or in debt. I didn't want to get snow in my undies. I didn't want to be stuck in France in a hospital in a full-body cast. I had never been skiing in my life (for good reason) and it was very unlikely I would be any good at it — I have the coordination of a baby giraffe on roller-skates and, being tall, any falls were likely to be large and spectacular and from a great height. And hurt. A lot.

No thanks.

There are dozens of reasons (a.k.a. excuses) you might have for not following through with the goals on your Life List. I call these reasons (a.k.a. excuses) the 'resisting forces'.

Some of your resisting forces will feel like a 10 km high, 10 000 km wide fence that is absolutely insurmountable. Other resisting forces might appear to be speed humps or mere road blocks that you could navigate your way around if you really put your mind to it ... but who can be bothered?

The combined pressure of all my resisting forces absolutely stopped me in my tracks when it came to the Great Ski Adventure. I was left standing still. Sir Isaac had me pegged. Game over. What's on Netflix?

The trick, I discovered, is to call the elephant in the room right at the very start of The Master Every Moment Framework — as soon as you identify your goal, the very next step you must take is to jump into the boxing ring with your brain and go 12 rounds over the resisting forces. Get them all out on the mat.

Let's get into a pretty comprehensive discussion of resisting forces to help you recognise some of the crappy self-talk our brains go on with. The examples I give are by no means exhaustive — I am sure that your crafty brain can come up with a few more curly ones to keep you firmly in the 'standing only' zone.

What might stop you — the resisting forces

I classify the resisting forces into two buckets: the Fear Bucket and the Lack Bucket. Both are bullies.

The Fear Bucket

Fear is a primal human emotion in reaction to danger, real or perceived. Fear can drive a physical reaction (for example — run away) and it can drive an emotional reaction. The fears I am focusing on here are those that elicit an emotional reaction, where we may not feel the physical need to flee from an experience, but we may very intensely experience a visceral reaction that makes us instinctively withdraw from or reject an experience.

FEAR OF FAILURE

Sometimes a fear of failing to achieve success can be enough to stop us going after the big-ticket, life-changing goals. Sometimes that fear can be enough to stop us going after some of the easier goals too.

I want you to sit with this one and really think it through. Are you reluctant to plan out and live out your Life List because you are worried that you might get it wrong? Or not quite right? Or not perfect enough?

Or are you worried that you might inadvertently leave something out? Or that there are too many choices and it's just too hard to think about?

That you might fail?

If this fear is one of your resisting forces it might well stop you chasing down your goals.

You might simply let life happen to you. Or you might wait for opportunities to land in your lap. Or you might set the bar so low that it's virtually impossible not to succeed.

Stop being that person.

Fear of failure has always been a big one for me. I am a high performer. I like to succeed and do things well, and I gain a lot of validation from that success. Success is a strong driving force for me. But the uncomfortable flip side to the success coin is the ever-present fear—what if I don't succeed this time? What if I fail?

Over time, and with the benefit of living 53 years and slowly gaining in wisdom, I know that my Life List and your Life List and The Master Every Moment Framework are not underpinned by outright success or outright failure. They are underpinned by opportunity and determination and love and a desire to live our absolute best lives.

And when you look at it this way, there is no such thing as failing when it comes to *designing* and *doing* your Life List. You have already succeeded simply by turning up with a desire to be more 'you'.

One of the very first Life List goals I set myself was to swim in the sea every single day—rain, hail or shine—for a full 12 months. Without a wetsuit. I was to swim with my two sisters (who were already four months into their swimming quests), which was going to be super helpful when it came to accountability and making me turn up.

The goal fully met all four of my Life List Rules — it was:

1. Glorious: because it was absolutely audacious

2. Challenging: it would challenge me physically and mentally (and, as it turned out, emotionally and spiritually)

3. Outside my comfort zone: god yes

4. New: yep.

I was petrified (you will read more about this later in Section IV of this book under 'S is for Swim'), but I approached the quest with the mindset that I would take it one swim at a time — one moment at a time. While I occasionally allowed myself to think about how proud I would be when I hit day 365, I rarely thought about the following day and absolutely never thought about getting through the following week — especially in the heart of winter.

So, what happened?

Well, in that first year of my goal I swam about 330 days out of 365. To be honest, I stopped counting.

Do I see that as failure? As not having succeeded? As letting myself down? As it not being quite as perfect as it could have been?

Absolutely fucking not. I see it as setting a goal that allowed me to swim 330 or so more days in a year than I would have ever swum had I not set the goal. And I have kept swimming — I am a few years in and I swim almost every single day.

For now, the point is — you cannot fail. You are already a winner.

FEAR OF OTHER PEOPLE THINKING YOU ARE SELFISH (AND LET'S JUST THROW IN A LITTLE GUILT TOO, JUST TO ROUND THINGS OFF...)

'Who is watching my journey? What are they thinking about the goals I'm setting for myself? Do they think I'm self-indulgent? Do they think I'm selfish? Are they talking about me? Maybe I shouldn't chase this next goal down...Oh god, and now I feel guilty...maybe I should just pop that goal on hold and be a better mother, partner, daughter, sister, employee, friend...'

Think of all of the women that you know personally and think hard as to whether any of them is someone you would classify as genuinely selfish. I can't think of one. Pretty much all of the women I know are selfless—regardless of whether they are mums, or women without children, or women who are in relationships, or women who are single, or any possible combination of partnered or not with kids or not—every woman I know is a giver.

Reflect on your own life and think about this properly. Think of everything you give to others, the time you invest in others, the work you do for others, the sacrifices you make for others. Do you really think that taking some time back now, for yourself, makes you selfish?

I don't.

I am the mum of three magnificent children. I love them more than life itself and my life has been enriched beyond imagination by being their mum.

But let's have a reality check here.

I had three babies in three and a half years. My darling children, like all children, are essentially blood-sucking vampires in a cuter form.

Research suggests that each pregnancy can age a mother's cells up to two years—which means that my children have literally taken six years from my life. Probably more when you add up all of the sleepless nights. They are the reason that I spent five years straight either pregnant and/or breastfeeding. They ruined my pelvic floor—I have not been able to sneeze in public since I was 30. They are the reason that my breasts no longer bounce, why my hair started to go grey in my 40s, why I have completed the final year of high school FOUR times (and only one of these was for myself), why I have a dodgy back, why I feel guilty if I put my phone on silent as I fall into bed exhausted at 8 pm when they are out on the town, why I have not gone one day in 23 years without doing a load of washing, why I have had my car at the panel beaters more times than I can count (and not because I was driving when the accident occurred, officer) and why I know exactly when the beat drops on some truly dreadful techno music. My oldest was born on my 30th birthday for god's sake, hence the reason I have not had even ONE day of the year that is dedicated solely to me for the last 23 years of my life.

And you want to call me selfish?

But to be honest, if anyone wants to label me in some way, then being a little selfish these days is a label that I am very prepared to wear with pride. Because it's my turn. I am very satisfyingly and very swiftly moving into the phase in my life where I get to experience the exquisite joy of becoming unapologetically selfish. And it is magnificent.

Don't let the door hit you on the arse as you get out of my way, my loves.

And, while I am on a roll, let's just debunk the whole 'guilt' thing while we are at it. As women we carry around so much guilt. We wear it like a shiny little badge of honour pinned directly and painfully onto our hearts. The more we bleed as we pin that badge on, the better.

I have thought and written extensively about guilt over the years and it genuinely does my head in. I write about it a little more in **Step 4: Identify What You Most Value**. At a rational level you know you are not doing yourself any favours by feeling guilty and that it really is time to let the guilt go. But that's the problem isn't it? Guilt often isn't rational.

If you are feeling a level of guilt about 'indulging' in designing and living your best life, I want you to try and reframe. Because, as well as performing multiple roles in your life that might include being a mum, a partner, a daughter, a sister, a friend, a colleague, an employee, an employer, a manager, an aunt and so on—the fact is that before you play any of these roles, first are foremost you are an individual. A standalone, unique person with individual wants, needs, emotions, feelings, thoughts and desires.

Tap into her—that individual—and ask her what she wants for the rest of her life, just for her.

Think about the whole 'fit your own oxygen mask first' analogy—it might sound trite but the fact is that it is an oft-repeated analogy for a reason—because *it's true*. Prioritising yourself from time to time allows you to fill your own cup. It creates peace and energy and contentment and happiness and fulfilment, which in turn allows you to continue to give to others without feeling depleted or frustrated or tired or used or like you are constantly running on empty.

Stop being so selfless. It's time to be a little selfish.

If it makes you feel better and if it will help you to indulge in a little *me first* without guilt, then go ahead and work with the other people in your life to create separate Life Lists as a family, or as a couple, or as a business owner or whatever the case may be.

But for now, know that you have given enough. Right now, at this moment, you have no more fucks to give. It's your turn.

FEAR OF BEING JUDGED FOR YOUR GOAL CHOICES

Judged by your partner. Judged by your kids. Judged by your friends. Judged by your mother or mother-in-law. Judged by your siblings. Judged by your colleagues. Judged by the cashier at the supermarket. The list goes on.

Yes, there are a lot of people out there with a seemingly endless amount of time to think about and openly share, to your face, their opinion on how you choose to live your life. God love them.

And they may well want to judge you on your Life List and the goals you set.

This one is simple. They don't need to know. This is your Life List. It's not your 'Marriage Life List' or your 'Family Life List' or your 'Life List for me and the chick on the checkout'. If you are surrounded by judgy people, even if you love them or kind of like them sometimes or flat out don't like them at all, you don't have to share any of this with them.

Why give them a chance to rain on your parade? Let them go and shit on their own parade.

FEAR OF DECLARING A LIFE FOR YOURSELF

If you are married or in a long-term relationship or have other significant people in your world, you might be fearful of creating space in your life that is just for yourself, separate from your life with others. You might fear upsetting this other person or people. You might fear them thinking that you are abandoning them or questioning your partnership or relationship with them. You might fear hurting them. You might fear angering them.

Communication is key.

First you need to talk to yourself and work out exactly what is it that you want and why you want it. You need to go back to the 'fitting your own oxygen mask first' analogy and understand that when you are at your best as an individual, you can be at your best for your most important relationships.

Second, you need to talk to your partner or other significant people and frame your desire for personal growth in such a way that others feel secure in your relationship and are excited for you and able to support your growth.

The Lack Bucket

None of us has the benefit of endless resources or intellect or skills. We all lack (to various extents) the wherewithal to make life supremely easy, seamless and absolutely effortless. Sometimes the things we lack don't present a barrier in chasing after our goals—we create a workaround and we get on with it. But sometimes what we lack seems to be so insurmountable that it can stop our goals in their tracks. So. Let's flush them out and, hopefully, put them to rest or at least create some actionable workarounds for what we might lack.

LACK OF A FRAMEWORK

'I don't know where to start or how to do this or how I will know when I have succeeded or how high I should set the bar or ...' Stop. I am sharing my proven frameworks with you, and so the 'I don't have a framework' resisting force is an excuse no longer. Magic!

LACK OF THE RIGHT MINDSET

So many women I work with have never set goals prior to working with me. And I think these women are incredible because the success they have achieved to date in their lives is through sheer hard work, sometimes being in the right place at the right time, or being tapped on the shoulder, or seeing an opportunity and having the guts to jump at it.

But here's the rub—imagine how much more they could have achieved over the course of their lifetimes if they had crafted a shit-hot, amazing, audacious set of goals each and every year, every step of the way, and created additional opportunities for themselves?

Yes, I absolutely want you to work hard and seize the opportunities that come your way, but please, please, please do this hand in hand with also taking the time to create and design your own destiny.

Years ago I worked in the corporate world as a lawyer. I worked extremely hard. I turned up, I contributed and I was offered opportunities. And I was doing pretty well—I could quite easily have stayed on that path of working hard and waiting to be recognised and rewarded or in the right place at the right time. Or I could take things into my own hands, because quite frankly the former road is harder and slower and a hell of a lot less fun.

And so I carved out time to think about exactly who I wanted to work for in that massive organisation (a progressive, incredibly well-regarded woman who reported to the COO and who was a billion levels higher than me on the totem pole), why I wanted to work for her (because she was a progressive, incredibly well-regarded woman who reported to the COO and who was a billion levels higher than me on the totem pole) and the gap in her existing structure that I felt needed to be filled. By me.

I put a proposal together and arranged a meeting with her and I gave her my pitch and she must have liked my chutzpah because she gave me the job. The actual job I had designed for myself.

And then I continued to work extremely hard and kept pitching my ideas to her.

One day as I sat working in my office she put her head around the door and asked me to come to a meeting with her and to bring my jacket. I had no time to prepare or gather myself as we entered the elevator and she hit the button for the executive floor. We were going to meet her boss, the COO and right-hand man to the CEO, and I was to pitch to him my idea for reducing costs associated with compliance-based training for operational staff.

Now this man had a reputation for suffering no fools. Of course I was terrified.

But I seized my chance and I made the pitch and he liked it and he gave me approval on the spot to change the entire way the organisation of 30 000-plus employees managed compliance-based training. And I did the work and it worked. And so I pitched him other ideas and he gave me more chances and I worked hard and those chances worked too.

I ended up working directly for him on special projects — he called me his 'keeper' because he said nothing ever got past me — and for the two years I worked for him I received two separate pay increases of 17 per cent and I was invited to participate in the executive talent program and I loved every minute of it.

Life by design, baby.

IMPOSTER SYNDROME

Ahhh, good old 'I'm not good enough, smart enough, fun enough, spontaneous enough, rich enough, pretty enough, thin enough, young enough, old enough, resilient enough, experienced enough, connected enough, enough enough'.

It's time to let this one go. I have.

Being 50ish helps. I care so much less about what other people think of me — I am not looking to prove myself to anyone any more and that mindset generates a dazzling level of freedom. I don't want to be better than you and I simply do not care if you are better, smarter, funnier, prettier, slimmer, fitter, groovier or richer than me. I honestly could not give a flying fuck. Life is too short. And I am sure as hell not going to sit around wasting my precious time on any of that shit.

The day you lose the impulse to agonise over whether you are enough enough for everyone around you, is the day you stop wasting your time on what you cannot control.

If you are finding the Imposter Syndrome hurdle a little harder to get over, then I would love for you to take a solid batch of time, two to three hours, to gather the data. Because any feelings of inadequacy or of being an imposter are exactly that—they are *feelings*. And we don't judge ourselves based on feelings—you, lady, need the *facts*.

In your beautiful Life List Planner (which you have printed out from my website at www.katechristie.com.au) there is a page for you to fill in the 4 Imposter Syndrome Quadrants where you are going to write a phenomenally long list of facts to challenge any feelings of inadequacy driven by a sense of Imposter Syndrome.

The 4 Imposter Syndrome quadrants are:

1. *My Wins.* This will be the longest list and the one you will add to most often—every day, in fact. I want you to list every win you have had over the last 1/2/5/10 years—you choose how far back you want to go. Your list should be wins both big (awards, public recognition, big project/client wins, etc.) and small (one of the kids vacuumed the house without you even asking).

2. *My Skills.* Write down all of your learned skills (the degree/s, diploma/s, the touch typing course you did when you were 15, the language you are learning on the side, any coaching you have received, programs you have participated in) and a list of your learned experiences—time in a role or tasks you have performed that have equipped you with a skill set you didn't previously have.

3. *My IP.* Write down a list of the talents you were born with—the god-given awesome stuff that is just easy for you to do. I call this my IP (intellectual property). Your talents will be the things that you are really, really good at, but that you often don't rate because you take them for granted. These will be the things that others

compliment you on and which you have previously dismissed because you think—'but doesn't everyone know how to do that?' No, they don't. Write them down.

4. *My Growth*. Write down a list of the errors or mistakes or learnings you have experienced that have helped you grow. This will include the things you didn't know, didn't do or didn't say that you wished you had, or the times you did not show up as your best self. The things on this list aren't failings—they are a gift, because you learned from the experience and you grew.

Look at the 4 Imposter Syndrome Quadrants often. Every time the Imposter Syndrome gremlin rears its ugly head, get those quadrants out and read every single thing on that big, long list. Use them as a tangible reminder that you are amazing, that you are enough, and that when it comes to creating your Life List and chasing after your goals, you have a track record for killing this stuff.

LACK OF AUTONOMY

You may have people around you—parents perhaps—who set you on a path designed to fulfil their expectations, goals and aspirations, and not yours. That path they mapped out for you might be influenced by cultural and family traditions.

This challenge is so very real for many. And the reality is that often this path is not the one you would have chosen for yourself. You might have had different goals and dreams. Maybe, just maybe, if you haven't already fully asserted your right to control your own destiny, today might be the day to start?

I once coached a very successful businesswoman who was completely in charge of her own incredible life in every respect except for family expectations about her role. While her parents and parents-in-law were proud of her achievements in the business community, there was a simmering secondary conversation that her business world was in some way a 'hobby' that they allowed her to indulge in, while her real role was that of homemaker, mother and wife.

Despite the fact that this woman earned an enormous income, far more than her husband's, there was a clear expectation from the senior women in her family that she should also be the fulltime cook and cleaner for her husband and children.

To avoid any direct conflict with these powerful older women, this otherwise phenomenally confident and extraordinarily competent woman would set the coffee table with a teapot and cups each time the cleaner came to clean her home—so that she could quickly sit down with the cleaner and pretend to be having a cup of tea with a friend if someone from her family dropped by.

The rub between choosing between your professional success and family expectations and harmony is very real for many. And while I acknowledge it and in no way can solve it in one page of this book, I urge you to use your beautiful brains and well-honed powers of negotiation to start a dialogue with those you love most who may well be holding you back.

Maybe it's time to break the cycle of tradition or cultural norms or family expectations. Maybe it's time to start putting yourself and your goals first. If not for you, then at least think about having the hard conversations so that the path will be easier for your own daughters.

LACK OF DISCIPLINE

I'm not even going to entertain this one. This ride isn't for the faint-hearted. You already know you don't lack self-discipline, or focus or willpower. You know you have a simmering, if not burning, desire to do things differently, to design what the rest of your life looks like. You already know you yearn to live an audacious life. How? Because you picked this book up and you chose to read it. You are here. You turned up. You must want this. And hell, sister—this ride is going to be a blast.

LACK OF MONEY

I have quite a few thoughts on this one. So here they are in no particular order and I hope some or all of them help you deal with this particular resisting force.

Not all of us have a bottomless pit of money—but if you do, I say this—*Hell yes, well done sister, you are killing it. Have fun. Spend it. Go big or go back to bed. But because you have a load of money, if you do choose to go back to bed (which I strongly urge you not to) then make sure it's a really lovely bed with the best possible linen money can buy.*

Not everything on your Life List will involve money. In fact, to ensure you have a beautifully integrated life, there should be a lot on your Life List that does not involve spending or accumulating money. Your Life List is designed to work across the 7 Life List Chapters, where you identify everything you most want to do for the rest of your life, including changing or adopting new behaviours or habits, or working on your health and wellbeing, or learning and growing, or the giving and sharing of your time and expertise, and so on. And many of these Life List goals won't cost you a cent. So, if money is an issue for you right now—then focus on the goals that fall within the Life List Chapters that are free.

Some things on your Life List will cost money—particularly items involving travel, adventures and experiences. You don't have to do all of these things at once. It's a Life List designed to help you identify what you most want to do and experience over the course of the rest of your life, it's not a Month List. One way to make the money last is to prioritise a money-related goal once a year or once every two years.

Start a Life List bank account and, rather than buying 15 coffees a week, buy five and deposit the money you save into your new Life List bank account and watch that money grow.

You may have a partner and/or family and the thought of dipping into the partnership/family savings for a little me time may feel self-indulgent, and the 'fear of people thinking I am selfish' monster may rear its ugly head (see the Fear Bucket). This one requires great communication between you and your partner. Explain why the goal is important to you. Maybe cost it out and agree that your partner can dip into the savings for an equal spend of money for one of their goals or wants. Maybe negotiate your use of that money this year and your partner's use of that money next year. Regardless of what level of creativity works for you and your partner, the key here is to communicate your needs, your partner's needs, and your common needs.

LACK OF TIME

I saved the best for last: *I don't have enough time.* As a time management specialist who has dedicated the last 10 years of her life to working with thousands of people around the world to help them reframe their relationship with time, the very simple fact is that we all — *every single one of us* — have all the time in the world.

The issue is not one of lacking time. The issue is where you choose to invest that time. And what I am asking you to do is to start investing some of your time in yourself.

● ● ●

Regardless of whether your resisting forces fall into the Fear Bucket or the Lack Bucket or both, the question you really need to ask yourself is this:

How bad do I want it?

When you deeply consider everything in the Fear Bucket and everything in the Lack Bucket you start to realise that the only thing that is holding you back from living your best life is—You. It's time to get out of your own way. Because if you really, really want it, if you really want to live an audacious life, if you genuinely want to make the next part of your life the absolute best it can be, then you will overcome the fear and you will overcome the lack (and Step 4: Identify What You Most Value will help big time) and it will be amazing.

I promise.

Take 30 seconds to identify the resistance you feel towards the goal you picked in Step 2. There is space next to each Goal in your Life List Planner to write down your resisting forces.

The Great Ski Adventure

My Resisting Forces

I had plenty. But my top three were:

1. Fear of being cold and wet: the idea of being cold and wet as a treat on a holiday was absolute anathema for me.

2. Fear of pain: I had never skied before. What if I hurt myself? What if I was laid up in a French hospital for 100 days in full body plaster?

3. Lack of money: I had no ski gear and no ski clothes. What on earth was I going to wear? And just how much was this going to cost me?

Well done. You are 50 seconds into your first MOMENT.

MOMENT

1. Set Your Intention
2. Pick a Goal
3. Identify Your Resisting Forces
4. **Identify What You Most Value**
5. Lock in a Deadline for the Goal

1. Mind Map the Goal
2. Lock in Deadlines for Each Action
3. Find Your Cheer Squad
4. Reframe Your Goal
5. Take a Step

MOMENTum

MOMENTous

1. Do It!
2. Celebrate
3. Share with the Squad
4. Acknowledge Your Growth and Lessons
5. Express Your Gratitude

4

Identify
What
You Most
Value

All things being equal, you can stop right now. You had a fleeting thought of something really cool to do, but the voice of reason chimed in like the bore that she is with a long list of very sensible resisting forces for why you are never, ever going to open that new door.

But we aren't quitters.

Thank god Sir Isaac Newton had a Third Law of Motion—'for every action there is an equal and opposite reaction'.

Now that you know what's likely to get in your way—the resisting forces—you need to counter these resisting forces with an equal or more powerful opposite positive force. Essentially—you need to knock those resisting forces out.

In **Step 4: Identify What You Most Value** you will take **30 seconds** to identify exactly what you most value in life—those powerful, motivational, positive forces of action that drive you forward.

The gift of guilt

When my kids were little and I was still a corporate chick flying up that ladder, lycra catsuit with an 'S' emblazoned across my insubstantial bosom hidden under my daywear, I had one of those crisis moments we have all faced—particularly women who juggle a career with any sort of carer responsibilities.

I had recently been nominated by my brilliant boss to participate in the executive leadership talent program and it was a huge honour with a huge associated workload and a huge investment by the organisation. The pressure was on.

At the time my kids were very young—two in the early years of primary school and one in kindergarten. My husband and I had a part-time nanny and the juggle was very real.

My kids were at that age and stage where we seemed to have a standing weekly appointment with the doctor. Whatever floor, table, fencepost or other kid they were licking at school or kindergarten quickly equated to 10 000 germs which flew into a full-blown tornado of temperatures, snot and misery at the speed of light. Generally speaking I would do morning duty, the nanny would do day duty, I would do afternoon duty and my husband and I would share night duty.

I was constantly switched on, constantly juggling, in a state of tangible stress, anxiety and guilt. If I was at work I was thinking about my kids. If I was with my kids I was thinking about work. It was hideous.

Weekends were sacred non-work zones for me. Except for one particular Sunday when I had to fly to Sydney for a four-day retreat for the new talent program. Of course, and because life has a way of testing us from time to time when we probably most need to be tested, my little boy was sick. He had come home from school on Friday complaining of a tummy ache. By Sunday morning he had a temperature and was sobbing in my arms because he didn't want me to go on my trip.

But I went.

And I will never forgive myself for that decision to prioritise my work and career and that stupid bloody talent program over my baby. Never. I will never forget driving away from the house and watching him in the rearview mirror looking so little and sad. It was heartbreaking. I still feel ashamed as I share this.

By late Sunday night my son's temperature was through the roof. My husband stayed up with him all night and I got on the first flight out of Sydney on Monday morning, having also had a sleepless night. The logistics were incredible. My husband was a lawyer and was due in court on Monday morning, so the nanny stayed with the two other children while my parents drove my sick son to the doctor where I met them in a taxi from the airport. Twenty minutes later we were in an ambulance on our way to the children's hospital where my son spent four days. And I barely left his side.

My guilt over that incident has been astronomical—scarring, jarring, consuming. As I write this 15 years later I am immediately transported back to the moment I drove away from that sad little boy and it makes me re-evaluate my decision all over again.

How could I have gotten it so wrong? How on earth could I have chosen work over my son? What the actual fuck was I thinking?

We have all had these moments in our lives. You don't get to be our age without some level of debilitating guilt for the choices we have made. For those times when we prioritised ourselves or made the wrong decision or even made the right decision but it went pear shaped and we lived to regret it.

I know I need to take my own advice on this one: no-one is going to give me a gold star for my guilt. I get it. But that memory has been hard to shrug off.

But what I have been able to do over the years is reframe that guilt—and I try now to see it as a gift. Because more than any other form of logical thinking or illogical thinking or emotion or feeling you ever experience, your guilt will often help you decide what it is in life that you most value along with the values by which you want to live.

That experience with my son was one of those moments.

What are my values?

Your core values are the set of principles that dictate the way you go about your life. Your core values are important when it comes to your Life List because they will dictate the way you go about implementing your list.

In every single professional, personal and self-development program you have *ever* undertaken in your lifetime you will have been asked to identify your core values. God only knows that you have done that exercise to death. So don't worry—we are not going to do it again. You are a grown up.

As an intelligent, driven and awesomely self-aware woman I am sure you have a pretty good handle on your core values and you are well aware that some of your core values may well change throughout your lifetime as your life circumstances change.

You know what your core values are. All I need you to do with them is keep them in mind and continue to honour them. Enough said.

What do I most value?

'What do I most value?' is a very different question altogether and it is quite possibly one that you have never asked yourself. This question is asking you to identify where it is you most want to invest your time (as opposed to the principles—your core values—that will guide your behaviour during that time investment).

Why is any of this important?

Because, put simply, after identifying your resisting forces in Step 2, this is the point in the whole goal-smashing process where many a less hearty gal would file her Life List away and go back to whatever it was she was doing before she momentarily flirted with the idea of doing something as awesome as prioritising herself for 10 minutes because it all suddenly seemed a bit too hard because there were a load of things in her Fear Bucket and quite a few things also spilling out of the Lack Bucket and ... breathe.

Getting the answer to this second question—what do I most value—is a critical step in The Master Every Moment Framework because you are going to use this knowledge to bulldoze your way through the resisting forces you identified in Step 2.

When I analysed the process I went through to get myself onto that bloody ski lift in France, the one thing that helped me absolutely blow the smithereens out of my resisting forces (and trust me, there were more resisting forces than just the ones I have shared with you) was the simple fact that my daughter wanted me to be there with her.

And so I reflected on this reality and here is a slightly edited and seriously sanitised version of my thought process at the time:

Remember that time you chose work over your son and he ended up in hospital for four days a very sick little boy and how he cried at 2 am when they tried to find a vein to hydrate him with a drip and how you have never, ever forgiven yourself to this day because you got it so very wrong? (... self-recrimination, self-recrimination, swear word, swear word, agony, agony, etc., etc.)

Remember how you prioritised your work and your ego over your sick child who you value more than anything in the world and how you have never, not once, since that day put work or yourself before the health, happiness, security and safety of your kids? (... self-recrimination, self-recrimination, swear word, swear word, etc., etc.)

Isn't prioritising your daughter—who you have missed terribly and who has literally cried on the phone to you for many, many hours—so much more important than all of the things you have identified as roadblocks such as being cold, wet, in pain, with snow in your undies, etc.? (You crazy... self-recrimination, self-recrimination, swear word, swear word, etc., etc. woman.)

And that was enough to help me reframe and push through my resisting forces.

Take 30 seconds to work out exactly what you value most in the world.

1. There are three questions I ask my clients to help them identify what they most value:

   » *If you were really, really sick, what would you get out of bed for?*

   » *When you are with your besties, that brilliant group of people who make your heart sing, what do you love talking about?*

   » *If you were to receive a compliment(s) from the person you most admire in this world, what would you love for them to say about you?*

2. It's likely that for each of these questions you will have many answers. Write them all down.

3. Put a circle around any answer that is common for all three questions. You might have 10 things that are common to all three questions. You might have five. It really doesn't matter. Essentially, these provide a very good indication of what you most value in your life.

4. There is a section under each goal in your Life List Planner to write down the things you most value that are relevant to helping you achieve that goal.

The things that you most value are an incredibly powerful and massively motivating source of inspiration every time you come up against a resisting force that threatens to stop you in your tracks. Boom!

Well done. You are 80 seconds into your first MOMENT.

The Great Ski Adventure

What do I value most?

It is time to eliminate the resisting forces by identifying exactly what I most value in the world—what would smash through the resistance?

This is easy. There are consistently three things I value most in the world: my kids and family; my business; and my health and wellbeing.

- My kids: I have not seen my daughter for five months. I have spent many, many hours with her on the phone with her sobbing and with me not being able to take away her anguish. And here she is wanting to go skiing with me. This is an amazing opportunity to experience something completely new together. No brainer.

- My business: I am about to launch my fourth book: *Me First: The Guilt-Free Guide to Prioritising You*, which is a time management book all about finding an extra 30-plus hours of time a month. Going to France and skiing for the first time in my life will provide huge fodder for my business articles, posts and speaking engagements. It also means that if I do not act I am at risk of being an absolute hypocrite. No brainer.

- My health and wellbeing: fresh air, exercise, awe, inspiration, French Alps. Another no brainer.

MOMENT

1. Set Your Intention
2. Pick a Goal
3. Identify Your Resisting Forces
4. Identify What You Most Value
5. **Lock in a Deadline for the Goal**

1. Mind Map the Goal
2. Lock in Deadlines for Each Action
3. Find Your Cheer Squad
4. Reframe Your Goal
5. Take a Step

MOMENTum

MOMENTous

1. Do It!
2. Celebrate
3. Share with the Squad
4. Acknowledge Your Growth and Lessons
5. Express Your Gratitude

5 Lock in a Deadline for the Goal

In **Step 5: Lock in a Deadline for the Goal,** I want you to take **10 seconds** to pick a deadline for the Go Big Goal you are working on and lock it into your calendar.

'Deadline': my second most favourite word

The email hit my inbox at 8 pm on Sunday night: 'Just a friendly reminder that your article for the magazine is due tomorrow.' Shit. I had completely forgotten about the article and, having spent 10 days straight writing 2000 words a day for this book, I had no more words to give.

Having just recently proclaimed during a speaking engagement that the word 'deadline' is my second favourite word in the world (behind the word 'moment') and that I was thinking of getting 'deadline' as my next tattoo (just kidding), the irony wasn't lost on me that I, the time management specialist for that publication, had almost let them down by forgetting my, ummm, deadline.

As I stayed up into the night to whip together the article I was very annoyed with myself. Not least because, just as 'deadline' is my second favourite word in the world, sleep is my most favourite activity in the world. This is the stuff I teach, for god's sake.

It didn't require deep reflection as to where I had slipped up. No soul-searching was required. I knew straight away where I had gone wrong: I hadn't set myself a deadline and I hadn't locked that deadline into my calendar.

Parkinson's Law is the economic theory that states that a task will expand to fill the time made available for it. We know this stuff. If you have a month to write the article it will take you a month to write the article. If you have two hours to write the article it will take you two hours to write the article. If you don't have a deadline to write the article, you won't write the article. Simple.

I divide deadlines into two separate categories:

- *External Deadlines*: These types of deadline are in the minority. These are the deadlines that are imposed on you by an external party or obligation: for example, a deadline imposed on you by your boss or a client—'I need this by 5 pm Thursday please'. External Deadlines are the easiest type of deadline to meet because there are consequences if you don't meet them. The huge rub here (as I personally experienced with the article for the magazine) is that you MUST also lock the external deadline into your calendar as a reminder to bloody turn up and get the bloody thing done.

- *Internal Deadlines*: These types of deadline are in the majority. These are the deadlines associated with a task where there is no external influence or obligation. These are the deadlines that you must drive for yourself. For these types of tasks if you don't impose a deadline and lock that deadline into your calendar, then you run the risk that you simply won't turn up and prioritise doing the task. The task will make its way to the bottom of your to-do list, or worse still, it will make its way into your too-hard basket where it will shrivel up and die a lonely death. Or you will procrastinate and do a thousand other things first. Or maybe you will kind of start it and jump in and out of it for a while. Or you will decide to put it off until inspiration strikes, or you have the energy, time, headspace or the right tools that require a trip to the shops or...I'll just do it later.

But what if later is too late?

There is only ever going to be one perfect time to start ticking off the items on your Life List: today.

Take 10 seconds to pick a deadline for the Go Big Goal you are working on and lock it into your calendar.

In terms of all of the other goals in your Life List:

- Go Now Goals are those acts of spontaneity where the time is right, the opportunity is there and you just jump—now!

- Go Small Goals will have shorter deadlines because they don't require as much planning or they are easier to achieve. I aim to complete at least one Go Small Goal every month or so.

- Go Big Goals will have deadlines that are further out.

There is space in your Life List Planner under each goal to write down your deadline for completing the goal. You can pencil each deadline in as you create your Life List (I have done this with some of my goals—you can see this in Section IV) or you can write the deadline in once you decide that this is a goal you want to prioritise.

The Great Ski Adventure

My deadline: 24 January 2020

Congratulations—you have completed your first MOMENT! It's time for some MOMENTum.

MOMENT

1. Set Your Intention
2. Pick a Goal
3. Identify Your Resisting Forces
4. Identify What You Most Value
5. Lock in a Deadline for the Goal

1. Mind Map the Goal
2. Lock in Deadlines for Each Action
3. Find Your Cheer Squad
4. Reframe Your Goal
5. Take a Step

MOMENTum

MOMENTous

1. Do It!
2. Celebrate
3. Share with the Squad
4. Acknowledge Your Growth and Lessons
5. Express Your Gratitude

It's MOMENTum time.

'Momentum' is defined as 'the measurement of mass in motion'—simply put—any object that is moving has momentum.

Sporting teams and athletes and corporate teams universally use the word 'momentum' to describe the feeling and pace they generate when they string together a series of successful steps to create wins.

In order to generate these wins, they simply need to constantly be moving forward.

And this is exactly the same when it comes to implementing the goals on your Life List—you need to be constantly moving forward to create a sense of momentum. Any object that is moving has momentum—all you need to do to generate that momentum in your life is to start moving. And once you start moving, it becomes easier to keep moving.

Having completed Part 1: MOMENT, you are already moving. Part 2: MOMENTum is designed to keep you moving—with intent, focus, passion and discipline. There are five steps in Part 2: MOMENTum, which will ensure you build a massive sense of forward momentum. You, my friend, are unstoppable.

MOMENTum

the measurement of mass in motion

MOMENTum

How I found momentum

Speed dating was definitely not on my Life List. But there I was at a bar on a school night well after my normal bed time, waiting for a message to pop up on my phone telling me who would be my first eight-minute date.

Having gone up to the barman to claim my first complimentary drink of the night I cast a nervous look around the pub. Just like a high school dance, the girls all gravitated to one corner and the boys to another. In all honesty I would have been very happy to stay in the girl corner and make friends with the women. There was a lot to learn and these women were all over it. They explained the rules of the game and pointed out which men were regulars on the whole speed dating circuit.

What? There's a circuit? There are regulars? Can I leave before it starts?

But before I could even contemplate making my escape my phone pinged and a picture of 'Giles' (obviously not his real name) popped up, rudely interrupting my chat with the nice, safe women.

After what can only be described as a cross between a treasure hunt without a map and a game of hide and seek, I lost a good two of my eight minutes trying to find Giles, who was skulking behind a tall palm clearly expecting me to find him rather than making any effort at all to join in on the game. Thanks a hell of a lot Giles — I have literally just put my face in the face of every bloke here to ask him if his name is Giles.

What ensued was six minutes of awkward chitchat with me asking Giles a lot of questions about himself and Giles not asking one question at all about me. Brilliant.

Six minutes later my phone flashed again to confirm that my date with Giles was, mercifully, over and that it was time to hunt down my next eight-minute date with 'Miles' (not his real name either). Miles was sitting in the corner like the king of the cool cats, also expecting women to come forth and worship him, and he spent all eight minutes talking about himself, with absolutely no prompting or questions required from me at all. It was simply a Miles Monologue. What a catch.

And so on and so forth for eight dates of eight-minute durations. I was exhausted after date three.

It was an excruciating but hilarious lesson in humility and satisfied three of my four goal criteria:

1. Challenging: tick

2. Outside my comfort zone: absolutely

3. New: god yes.

And it was all in aid of achieving my actual current Life List challenge, which was to say 'yes' for a whole month to every opportunity that presented itself. My cheeky friend who knew about my Yes Quest had immediately served up an invitation for me to join her for speed dating, knowing full well that it was not within my capacity to decline (more on that in Section IV under 'Y is for Yes Quest').

Activities that also got caught up in my Yes Quest included:

*   going out dancing

*   agreeing to book to hike The Overland Trail in Tasmania (more on that in Section IV 'H is for Hiking')

*   sound healing (more on this one in Section IV under 'W is for Woo Woo')

*   plunging 30 m down a waterslide (more on that one in Section IV under 'Y is for Yes Quest')

*   seeing a clairvoyant (more on this one in Section IV under 'W is for Woo Woo').

By my nature, I am a homebody.

And while I love setting myself goals, I have in the past done so under fairly well controlled, science lab-ish, quality controlled conditions, which includes lots of planning, clarity about my schedule, and control over the process. I generate the idea for what I want to do and then I go do it.

As I write this I do recognise that I sound every bit the control freak that I am, but here's the thing—I completely recognise this, which is why I set myself the Yes Quest goal in the first place.

I had no real intention or hope of genuinely enjoying any of the Yes Quest activities—and so knew I was unlikely to satisfy my 4th Life List Rule that the goal be 'glorious'. Instead, the Yes Quest was primarily about pushing myself well out of my comfort zone, where I had for far too long been residing.

But I was very, very wrong. It was a blast!

I experienced two big learnings from my Yes Quest.

First, while the activities I took part in very clearly met three of my four Life List Rules and I would never, ever in a million years, have done any of them voluntarily or with any sense of enthusiasm if not for the Yes Quest challenge, each and every one of them turned out to be absolutely glorious—hence unwittingly also meeting my 4th Life List Rule. Each activity was either glorious in and of itself (dancing was always going to be glorious and it was) or glorious because I was so damn proud of myself for turning up and putting myself out there (such as speed dating).

Second, my sense of enthusiasm for the Yes Quest became contagious and self-fulfilling. The more I said yes, the more fun I had, which made me say yes to the next quest which led to more fun which—drum roll…led me to actually go looking for opportunities that I would previously never have explored, all so that I could throw them into the Yes Quest ring.

Who is this woman?

After three weeks of the Yes Quest my daughter said to me, 'Mum, something has changed about you. You seem so happy. You look amazing.'

And I was happy, and I did look amazing and more importantly I felt it. Something had definitely shifted.

I had momentum.

● ● ●

It's time to generate your momentum. You have everything you need—take a deep breath, take my hand, pick up your pen and let's jump into your future. Together.

MOMENT

1. Set Your Intention
2. Pick a Goal
3. Identify Your Resisting Forces
4. Identify What You Most Value
5. Lock in a Deadline for the Goal

MOMENTum

1. **Mind Map the Goal**
2. Lock in Deadlines for Each Action
3. Find Your Cheer Squad
4. Reframe Your Goal
5. Take a Step

MOMENTous

1. Do It!
2. Celebrate
3. Share with the Squad
4. Acknowledge Your Growth and Lessons
5. Express Your Gratitude

1 Mind Map the Goal

My sisters are incredibly creative and talented. My older sister has an interior design flair that I love and which, no matter how hard I try and emulate it, I cannot replicate. She can place four pot plants of varying sizes together in such a way that they look like they should be in the cover of *Vogue Living*; my attempt looks like four sad plants at a networking event that don't actually want to be there, let alone sitting together. My younger sister is in fashion and it is to her I turn for clothes and advice on what to wear each time I am forced to go anywhere that doesn't allow me to wear my kids' old school tracksuit pants.

I do not have the same creative flair.

My talents are far, far more in the process area: I'm the chick good at organising and planning and getting shit done.

And so you can imagine my absolute delight when I discovered liquid chalk—a life-changing invention by someone or other who is a genius and who should be right up there with whoever invented post-it notes.

Liquid chalk is pretty true to its name and comes in all the best bright colours to make your windows and mirrors look like virtual works of art when in reality all you have really done is plan out your schedule for the next six months.

Your first Life List goal that you identified in MOMENT: Step 2: Pick a Goal might at first feel a little daunting. It is, after all, a Go Big Goal and essentially this means that it is a big project. And unless you have great project-management skills, any big goal or project can feel overwhelming—where do I start, what do I do next, how should I sequence this, where is the cat, what do I need to get from the shops?…and we just lost you.

Which is exactly what we do not want, because this whole Life List thing is supposed to be inspiring and awesome and addictive and very, very doable.

This is where mind mapping comes in. Mind mapping is a brilliant strategy to help you break big goals down into smaller actions. Whether you choose to mind map using a mind mapping app, butchers paper, post-it notes, or, like me, liquid chalk, it's time to choose your tools of choice and break that big, audacious goal down into very doable bite-sized pieces.

How to mind map

In Step 1, you will Mind Map your goal. Using your tool of choice, write the goal you identified in MOMENT: Step 2 as a statement in a central position and put a circle around it. When I was planning the Great Ski Adventure I wrote 'Skiing in France'.

Identify the four or five or 18 key themes that spring to mind when you think about all of the moving parts that make up this goal. When I was planning the Great Ski Adventure the themes I identified included:

- Flights/Travel

- Ski Resorts

- Accommodation

- Food

- Equipment

- Itinerary.

Place each key theme around the central goal with plenty of room for writing the actions that drive off each theme.

Brain dump all of the actions you need to complete under each theme. When I was planning the Great Ski Adventure, under the Travel theme, for example, the steps I identified included:

- research airlines

- research air fares

- check visa requirements

- check baggage allowance

- sort out airport transfers

- research travel insurance including skiing insurance (I discovered there was in fact, such a thing—under 'extreme sports')

and so on. The bigger the goal, the more actions you will have on your mind map.

Under each goal in your Life List Planner there is space for you to mind map out all of the actions you will take to accomplish the goal.

The Great Ski Adventure

Mind map

You can see my mind map on the next page.

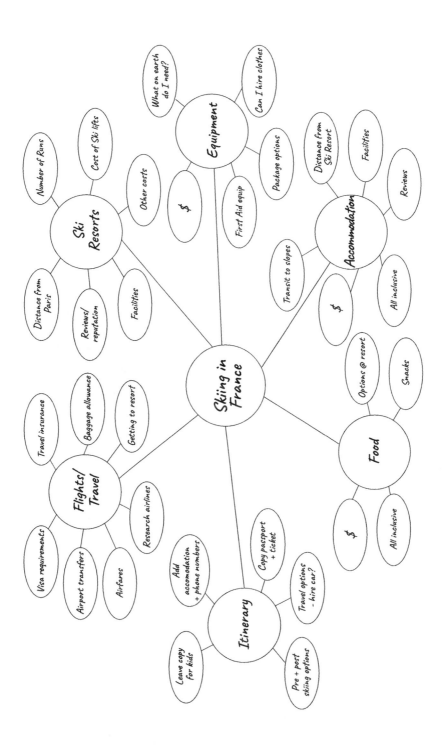

MOMENT

1. Set Your Intention
2. Pick a Goal
3. Identify Your Resisting Forces
4. Identify What You Most Value
5. Lock in a Deadline for the Goal

MOMENTum

1. Mind Map the Goal
2. **Lock in Deadlines for Each Action**
3. Find Your Cheer Squad
4. Reframe Your Goal
5. Take a Step

MOMENTous

1. Do It!
2. Celebrate
3. Share with the Squad
4. Acknowledge Your Growth and Lessons
5. Express Your Gratitude

2 Lock in Deadlines for Each Action

From MOMENT: Step 5: Lock in a Deadline for the Goal, you already well and truly understand the importance of setting deadlines and locking them into your calendar.

In Step 2, for every action you have identified in your mind map, I want you to lock in a standalone deadline.

When it comes to deadlines, other tips to keep in mind:

- *Batch your calendar.* I write and speak extensively about the productivity strategy called 'batching'. Batching is the concept of grouping like tasks together so that you complete them in one chunk of time—for example, you can batch together chunks of time to do all the tasks that require online research to achieve your goal.

- *Batch a weekly deadline.* To help maintain momentum, I then batch a weekly deadline (day and time) into my calendar to complete these like tasks together—for example, every Friday from 3 to 5 pm I might batch in 'Goal Research' as the deadline.

- *Batch a chunk of time per week.* I find goal setting and working towards my goals very stimulating and exciting, so I tend to batch at least two to three hours a week where I prioritise working on my goals.

- *Set up reminders and alarms.* In your calendar, use colours or stars or all caps or emojis or bells and whistles to make it very clear to your brain that these are non-negotiable deadlines that you will prioritise. You will set the deadline and you will turn up.

The Great Ski Adventure

Batched calendar

See the next page for my calendar.

	SUN	MON	TUE	WED	THU	FRI	SAT
8 AM		Research Flights 8–9am**	Travel Insurance 8–9am**	Ski Resorts 8–9am**	Ski Resorts 8–9am**	Ski Resorts 8–9am**	
9 AM		Work-High Value 9–9:45am Break, 9:45am	Work-High Value 9–9:45am Break, 9:45am	Work-High Value 9–9:45am Break, 9:45am	Work-High Value 9–9:45am Break, 9:45am	Work-High Value 9–9:45am Break, 9:45am	
10 AM		Work-High Value 10–10:45am Break, 10:45am	Work-High Value 10–10:45am Break, 10:45am	Work-High Value 10–10:45am Break, 10:45am	Work-High Value 10–10:45am Break, 10:45am	Work-High Value 10–10:45am Break, 10:45am	
11 AM		Work-High Value 11–12pm	Work-High Value 11–12pm	Work-High Value 11–12pm	Work-High Value 11–12pm	Work-High Value 11–12pm	
12 PM		Lunch, 12pm	Lunch, 12pm	Lunch, 12pm	Lunch, 12pm	Lunch, 12pm	
1 PM		Process driven work/Low Value Tasks	Process driven work/Low Value Tasks	Process driven work/Low Value Tasks	Process driven work/Low Value Tasks	Process driven work/Low Value Tasks	
2 PM		12:30–4pm	12:30–4pm	12:30–4pm	12:30–4pm	12:30–4pm	Equipment Hire 2–3pm**
3 PM							Equipment Hire 3–4pm**
4 PM							Book Flight 4–5pm**
5 PM							Book Accom 5–6pm**
6 PM		Accommodation 6–7am**	Accommodation 6–7am**	Accommodation 6–7am**	Accommodation 6–7am**	Accommodation 6–7am**	
7 PM							
8 PM							

MOMENT

1. Set Your Intention
2. Pick a Goal
3. Identify Your Resisting Forces
4. Identify What You Most Value
5. Lock in a Deadline for the Goal

1. Mind Map the Goal
2. Lock in Deadlines for Each Action
3. **Find Your Cheer Squad**
4. Reframe Your Goal
5. Take a Step

MOMENTum

MOMENTous

1. Do It!
2. Celebrate
3. Share with the Squad
4. Acknowledge Your Growth and Lessons
5. Express Your Gratitude

3 Find Your Cheer Squad

The decision to share my first Life List publicly was an act of spontaneity. I am an opinion columnist for *CEOWORLD Magazine* and, having drafted the first iteration of my Life List with the thoughts and feelings that came immediately to my mind direct from my heart—it took me only 20 minutes—I submitted the piece to the magazine on a whim. I actually didn't think they would publish it because it was very different to my usual commentary for them.

Pain and loss are incredibly private and, at least in my life, have always played out behind closed doors. But I had a compulsion to share that list with the universe—as part of my healing process but also because I thought that it might help others.

Importantly too, publishing that Life List was an act of celebration and resolution. By making that list public I was openly declaring to the world my determination to live a very different life from that moment on. It left me nowhere to hide. I was now accountable.

Publishing the list was an important lesson for me—a lesson that it's okay to let my guard down; to not always pretend that I am doing perfectly well thank you very much when in fact I am anything but; that sharing my truth doesn't push people away, it actually draws them in; and that being open and honest creates a community of people who instantly get you. The outpouring of support I received from that article blew me away.

In **Step 3** you will **Find Your Cheer Squad**, just like I did.

My cheer squad

As well as taking a step in healing myself and moving forward with conviction and trying to help others live their best lives, in sharing that article I had unwittingly created a cheer squad of amazing supporters—most of whom I don't know and will most likely never meet—who have my back, who are on my side, and who want to see me succeed.

Your support has and continues to overwhelm me and it drives me every single day to keep living my best life. My cheer squad—you—bring me so much joy when I hear from you that you have been inspired by my words to create and live out your own Life List.

But more than that—you keep me accountable. I cannot and will not let you down. You keep me motivated. You help me maintain my momentum. It is you I think of when I can't quite be bothered—because you have my back—and you make me be bothered again.

I can't tell you how honoured I continue to be by every single message I receive from you—like these.

> *Kate, this is uplifting, inspirational and plain old fabulous. And how comforting/funny that life proves time and again that new lives, loves, horizons and resolutions can spring from absolute devastation. Thank you for writing and sharing this—I'm going to think about my own list now.*
>
> **Kate Halfpenny**
>
> *Thank you Kate Christie. This resonated with me and I too will think about my own life's too short resolutions!*
> **Sue Ferguson**
>
> *What a great list. I might have to steal it.*
>
> **Natalie Coulson**
>
> *Thank you for sharing this and inspiring us with your truth.*
>
> **Sehr Ahmed**
>
> *Thank you for sharing Kate, I've actually saved your article to refer back to your list myself and to create my own as life really is too short. Thank you.*
>
> **Meghan Ede**
>
> *Thank you so much for sharing and sorry for your loss. It would be great to get a follow up article this time next year to see how this played out!*
> **David Grant**
>
> *Points we should all heed.*
>
> **Anil Utamchandani**
>
> *I love your list of things and absolutely will be doing the same myself. Take care—love and strength to you and your children xx*
> **Victoria Standring**

(continued)

YESSSS!!!!!! I'm recently single 52 and doing the same. Throwing myself into the art career I always wished I'd had and swimming (nearly) every day too. PS. Is it bad that forgoing vacuuming was my favourite thing on the list???

Sharon England

Your list has inspired me to try even harder. Thank you.

Christina Allen

You are an amazing role model to your kids and other young (and not so young) professionals.

Angela Sullivan

I'm inspired by your list and I will be referring to it frequently. Thank you!

Caitlyn Nguyen

Thank you Kate for reminding me what is important in life, and that life is too short to do the things that do not add value to my life.

Bonnie Qiu

I needed to hear these words, thank you.

Kamila Hutchinson

I bloody love this Kate Christie. Great inspiration for my own list. Thank you.

Monica Rosenfeld

'Value my values' This is to live by. Thank you for sharing Kate Christie a magnificent list of addition and subtraction. Wishing you all the best.

Dr Linda Wilson

There is a lot power in accountability. But I think there is far more power in having a supportive, nonjudgemental, all in, love you to the moon and back cheer squad.

How to find your cheer squad

You do not have to go for all out public accountability by writing an article and sharing it with the world or posting it on Facebook or taking out a billboard on the high street or buying advertising on the radio. All you need to do is have a gang you trust to cheer you on.

I mix my Life List goals up a lot. I have some Life List goals that are just me challenging myself and I complete them on my own. I have other Life List goals that I chase after with one or two or even a gang of girlfriends. In every case, however, I always have a cheer squad on my side.

In Step 3: Find your Cheer Squad—you might select your best friends, have a specific partner in crime who you know will always egg you on (and be there with the backup eggs), or tap into my private Facebook group specifically designed to give you a group of ready-made, like-minded women who want to live their best lives. Details on how to apply to join the group are on my website at www.katechristie.com.au.

You can select and implement your goals from your Life List on your own while tapping into the cheer squad for accountability, assurance, love and encouragement...or you can enlist your cheer squad to live out your selected Life List goal with you—choose a goal that is common to you all and chase it down together. Accountability, cheer squad and partners in crime all in one.

Actively keep your cheer squad up to date on your progress—you might decide to update them once a fortnight or every month or, for smaller goals, let them know what you have already achieved.

Generously cheer on the women around you. Give them a regular and enthusiastic 'Hell YESSS! You are a superstar!' every step of their journey. And when they are feeling low or slow or like they are going backwards, be there to pick them back up with a friendly shove in the right direction.

There is space in your Life List Planner under each goal to list your cheer squad for the goal.

The Great Ski Adventure

Cheer squad

My daughter. My dad. My sons (in retrospect my sons were pretty useless actually, although they did gain a lot of joy from the outcome...more on that later).

MOMENT

1. Set Your Intention
2. Pick a Goal
3. Identify Your Resisting Forces
4. Identify What You Most Value
5. Lock in a Deadline for the Goal

1. Mind Map the Goal
2. Lock in Deadlines for Each Action
3. Find Your Cheer Squad
4. **Reframe Your Goal**
5. Take a Step

MOMENTum

MOMENTous

1. Do It!
2. Celebrate
3. Share with the Squad
4. Acknowledge Your Growth and Lessons
5. Express Your Gratitude

4 Reframe Your Goal

You have set your intention to live an audacious life.

You have identified the goal you want to implement.

You have identified your resisting forces, and you have bulldozed through any resistance by clearly identifying and articulating what you most value in this world.

You have locked in the deadline by which you will complete the goal.

You have mind mapped that baby to within an inch of its life and you have allocated separate deadlines to each and every action you need to take to get to the starting line.

Your cheer squad is in place and may in fact be on the journey with you, rather than just on the sidelines going nuts with pom poms.

In **Step 4** you will **Reframe Your Goal** to make it as real as possible. The more realistic and tangible your goal, the more you can actually see it, feel it and touch it, then the more likely it is that you will turn up and achieve it. Reframing your goal firms up your intention and adds fuel to the fire of your momentum.

Like all good goals, your reframed goal must have three elements. It must:

1. be written in the present tense, like it has just happened today. This will help you visualise and even (if you believe in this) manifest the goal. When I think and act like something has already happened, it makes the doing so much easier.

2. be concrete — the more concrete the goal, the better the tools you have in place to smash it. A loosey-goosey goal such as: 'I want to eat better' simply won't cut it. You need to set yourself up for success by stating exactly why and how you are going to eat better, including how often you eat, what fruits and vegetables you will

incorporate into each meal, what a meal plan for the week looks like, the exercise you will undertake to accompany your new diet, and so on.

3. include a range of measures so that you are regularly completing small steps along the way (and so you can celebrate the journey), as well as being very clear on when you have crossed the finish line.

There is space in your Life List Planner under each goal to reframe your goal.

The Great Ski Adventure

Reframed goal

It's 24 January 2020 and I have just spent *3 days skiing with Peggy in France. I found an *all-inclusive package with accommodation, food, lift passes, skis, and clothes. *We skied every day from 9 am until 4 pm. I *quickly graduated from the beginner runs and I did not, at any stage, *get snow in my undies. I have *lots of content for my writing, I have *published my first article about my adventures, and *I will turn this whole experience into a framework that I can speak about, write about and share with my clients. *I am feeling healthy and alive and I LOVE skiing!

* = a measure

MOMENT

1. Set Your Intention
2. Pick a Goal
3. Identify Your Resisting Forces
4. Identify What You Most Value
5. Lock in a Deadline for the Goal

1. Mind Map the Goal
2. Lock in Deadlines for Each Action
3. Find Your Cheer Squad
4. Reframe Your Goal
5. **Take a Step**

MOMENTum

MOMENTous

1. Do It!
2. Celebrate
3. Share with the Squad
4. Acknowledge Your Growth and Lessons
5. Express Your Gratitude

5 Take a Step

We already know from Sir Isaac Newton that an object that is moving has momentum. In other words: YOU have to be moving to create momentum.

You have done all of the hard work. You have planned this out beautifully. What would otherwise normally be the hardest step in chasing any goal—taking action—is now the easiest step because you have set yourself up for success with all of the glorious prep work you have done.

Step 5 requires you to **Take a Step**. Just one step forward will help you generate momentum. For example, if your audacious goal is to run a marathon, then your very first step might be to walk 5000 steps today. If your audacious goal is to jump out of a plane, your very first step might be to google 'life insurance' (or maybe something like: 'What are the chances of my parachute not opening?').

And, just like the doctor's appointment or the meeting with a client that is locked into your calendar for tomorrow, you need to turn up and take that step.

So, let's get moving. Take that first step. Right now.

And, once completed, cross it off your mind map or update your spreadsheet or shade it on your calendar or cross it off your to-do list or do whatever it is that you personally do to mark the completion of a task. Personally, I add to my sense of momentum by physically crossing off each step from a to-do list.

Then turn up for the next step. Do it. Mark it off.

Then turn up for the next step. Do it. Mark it off.

And then…you have momentum.

The Great Ski Adventure

Take a step

My first step was a very small and simple one: I googled medical travel insurance.

That was it. Simple. Small. Doable. Forward movement.

My next step was to compare policies and read the small print to make very sure that in the event of a major injury I could be airlifted off the mountain or at the very least tucked into a sled with a fluffy blanket and dragged from the summit by a team of huskies.

My next step was to research ski resorts that were within four hours of Paris and which offered all-inclusive packages of accommodation, food, transfers, ski hire, ski clothes and ski lift passes. And I found one.

I was on a roll.

Congratulations—you have MOMENTum! It's time for something MOMENTous.

MOMENT

1. Set Your Intention
2. Pick a Goal
3. Identify Your Resisting Forces
4. Identify What You Most Value
5. Lock in a Deadline for the Goal

1. Mind Map the Goal
2. Lock in Deadlines for Each Action
3. Find Your Cheer Squad
4. Reframe Your Goal
5. Take a Step

MOMENTum

MOMENTous

1. Do It!
2. Celebrate
3. Share with the Squad
4. Acknowledge Your Growth and Lessons
5. Express Your Gratitude

And now you get to live a big, spectacular, enormous, incredible life where you create, generate, experience and manifest a life that is Momentous.

Referring to a goal or adventure or act or achievement as 'momentous' elevates that event to something of genuine significance—something that will have a lasting impact on your future.

Man landing on the moon was a momentous event. The creation of the internet was a momentous event. A baby taking her first steps is a momentous event.

You first kiss, your first love, your first loss, your first car, your first time driving a car on your own, your first house, your first trip without your parents, your first trip without your kids. All momentous.

Creating your Life List and living a life by design on your terms is momentous.

Part 3: MOMENTous is the final five steps of The Master Every Moment Framework—where you get to experience the goal, celebrate your success, reflect on the magnificence of your experience and what you have learned, and express what you are grateful for.

PART 3

MOMENTous

MOMENTous

of great or lasting importance or consequence

MOMENT

1. Set Your Intention
2. Pick a Goal
3. Identify Your Resisting Forces
4. Identify What You Most Value
5. Lock in a Deadline for the Goal

1. Mind Map the Goal
2. Lock in Deadlines for Each Action
3. Find Your Cheer Squad
4. Reframe Your Goal
5. Take a Step

MOMENTum

MOMENTous

1. **Do It!**
2. Celebrate
3. Share with the Squad
4. Acknowledge Your Growth and Lessons
5. Express Your Gratitude

1 Do It!

It's D-Day. In **Step 1** you need to turn up! **Do it**. Enjoy every second knowing that this one is for you. And oh my god, my brilliant friend you are magnificent.

The Great Ski Adventure

Do it!

Turns out the hardest part of the whole process was getting authorisation from the student exchange host agency to release my daughter two weeks ahead of schedule.

Happily, however, after proving that I had in fact birthed her and that I was very happy to resume full legal responsibility for her, she was released.

Our reunion on that freezing cold train platform in France was every bit as good as when Marlin finally finds Nemo.

And then we did it.

We spent three days skiing in France. It was MOMENTOUS!

MOMENT

1. Set Your Intention
2. Pick a Goal
3. Identify Your Resisting Forces
4. Identify What You Most Value
5. Lock in a Deadline for the Goal

1. Mind Map the Goal
2. Lock in Deadlines for Each Action
3. Find Your Cheer Squad
4. Reframe Your Goal
5. Take a Step

MOMENTum

MOMENTous

1. Do It!
2. **Celebrate**
3. Share with the Squad
4. Acknowledge Your Growth and Lessons
5. Express Your Gratitude

2 Celebrate

Congratulations! You did it. You are awesome!

In **Step 2** it's time to **Celebrate**. Change your celebrations up — sometimes it will be a little pat on your own back or high-five in the mirror, a long hot bath, a massage … or it might even be a full-blown party. Whatever works for you. For mine, well, one of my favourites is …

Dancing my arse off

The invitation was very clear — I was invited to the opening night of a 'dance club' — a neat little business started by a Melbourne woman who just wanted to dance with her friends with absolute abandon. The club would run from 7 pm to 9 pm; I didn't need to dress up (but could if I wanted); I should wear comfortable shoes (but if I wanted to wear heels I would be politely asked to remove them to protect the floor); and I was to bring a bottle of water.

This was no nightclub. There would be no-one watching or judging or raising their eyebrows at my dance moves or checking me out or trying to grind their pelvis into my unsuspecting bottom. There would be no need to wait until 1 am for the good music to start or to scream at each other over the booming beat or to place our handbags on the floor in the centre of our circle so we could dance and mind our belongings at the same time, or any of the other things I associated with a night out dancing in my youth.

This was a dance club for chicks just like me (and you) who want to dance their arses off with no-one watching, and then be home in bed by 9.30 pm.

And it was magnificent.

I arrived in my workout gear, very comfortable shoes, with a 2-litre bottle of water, and I danced for two hours straight. I have never in my life danced like that, safe in the knowledge that not one other person in that room could give a flying fuck about me because they were too far lost in their own little bubble of completely free dancing queen self-abandon. I was exultant. I only stopped dancing for three hurried trips to the bathroom, as my pelvic floor isn't exactly leak proof these days.

There is a power that comes with being a 50ish woman with no more fucks to give. A liberation that I can look like, dress like, act like and be whatever it is I want to be.

I cannot express how joyful it is to live this way. I want you to live in exactly the same way and I want you to celebrate your tenacity in exactly the way you want to celebrate it.

For me when I want to celebrate, I'm going to dance.

Celebrate your achievement

Even if the Life List goal you have completed is in itself a celebration of your life—for example, you might have just climbed a mountain, run a marathon, volunteered your time to plant a thousand trees, driven in a convertible around Italy, mentored a young businessperson—the point is that you need to acknowledge in some symbolic way that you have gone through a process where you:

- created your Life List

- set your intention to live a magnificent life

- chose a goal to focus on

- identified the resisting forces that might trip you up, slow you down, or stop you in your tracks

- pushed through the resistance by reminding yourself of what you most value in your life

- set yourself a deadline

- mind mapped out your goal, including all the little actions you needed to complete

- rallied your support team

- reframed your goal into something extremely tangible

- implemented each action and gained momentum

- actually completed the goal!

Setting and smashing your goals takes work and guts and determination and hustle and self-belief. Do not underestimate how incredible your achievement is. And it deserves to be celebrated. At the very least pat yourself on the back for a job bloody well done.

The Great Ski Adventure

Celebrate

On completing the Great Ski Adventure, which really was a celebration of life in itself, we took ourselves off to a very lovely posh dinner that involved an alarming amount of gooey cheese to celebrate my first (and last, but more on that later) ever ski trip. We reminisced and looked at our photos and we laughed until we cried and then we went back to the hotel to change the bandages (again, more on that later).

MOMENT

1. Set Your Intention
2. Pick a Goal
3. Identify Your Resisting Forces
4. Identify What You Most Value
5. Lock in a Deadline for the Goal

1. Mind Map the Goal
2. Lock in Deadlines for Each Action
3. Find Your Cheer Squad
4. Reframe Your Goal
5. Take a Step

MOMENTum

MOMENTous

1. Do It!
2. Celebrate
3. **Share with the Squad**
4. Acknowledge Your Growth and Lessons
5. Express Your Gratitude

3 Share with the Squad

In **Step 3: Share with the Squad** and soak up their praise and love
—because you deserve it.

In 2022 I walked the Larapinta Trail in central Australia (you can read
more about this in Section IV under 'H is for Hike'). It was an incredibly
gruelling experience that saw me walk 130 km in six days across a very
remote, hard, rock-strewn landscape and challenged me more than I could
have imagined on every possible level.

Hiking with a group of seven others provided amazing support and
camaraderie and we were literally each other's cheer squad every single
day—especially the day we were up at 3.30 am and walked 32 km.

But it was a mental image of my cheer squad at home that really kept
me going: the thought of how proud I would be to arrive home and have
my kids tell me how amazing I was for completing such an arduous
journey. Because it was arduous—I'm not going to lie, in my darkest
moments I fantasised a little about the welcome home celebrations
with my kids chanting my name and holding up signs as I was carried
from the plane.

The afternoon the hike ended I called my kids and revelled in their
admiration and cried when they told me how proud they were of me.
Reach out to your cheer squad and make sure you share the good, the
bad, the ugly and the overwhelming awesomeness of what you have
achieved. They are emotionally invested in your journey—they want
to see you succeed and they will be thrilled to bask in some of your
reflected glory.

The Great Ski Adventure

Share with the squad

My daughter, Peggy, was the best cheer squad ever, as well as my partner in crime. She encouraged me, stuck by my side while I learnt the basics, literally cheered for me as I made my first run, taught me how to get on ski lifts (those things don't stop for anyone), and encouraged me to try harder runs. She also enjoyed very much watching me take a good 15 minutes trying to click my bloody ski boot into the ski, filmed me falling over more times than I could count and laughed her arse off at how useless I was.

Watching the videos of me falling, the boys just laughed.

My dad mumbled something like 'That's how you bloody kill yourself...'

MOMENT

1. Set Your Intention
2. Pick a Goal
3. Identify Your Resisting Forces
4. Identify What You Most Value
5. Lock in a Deadline for the Goal

1. Mind Map the Goal
2. Lock in Deadlines for Each Action
3. Find Your Cheer Squad
4. Reframe Your Goal
5. Take a Step

MOMENTum

MOMENTous

1. Do It!
2. Celebrate
3. Share with the Squad
4. **Acknowledge Your Growth and Lessons**
5. **Express Your Gratitude**

4 Acknowledge Your Growth and Lessons

We already know that there is no failure in the Life List journey (see the discussion of fear of failure in MOMENT: Step 3: Identify Your Resisting Forces). We are living and existing in a purely success-based zone.

That doesn't mean that you won't make mistakes or that there won't be things that you could have done differently or better. It means exactly the opposite of that—it means that there will be mistakes and there will be things you could have done differently or better but you know that, and you are prepared to acknowledge any mistakes and learn and grow from them and try not to make them again.

In my book that makes you a winner.

There will also be lessons affirming how incredible you are, or reminding you of what is important to you, or helping you reflect on what you want to do more of or less of in the future.

Growth and lessons and acknowledging and recording them are key.

To cultivate and flex our 'growth and lessons learned' muscle, I have built Step 4 into The Master Every Moment Framework to ensure that we actively engage in some solid self-reflection on a regular and consistent basis. After you complete each goal on your Life List, reflect on what you have achieved. There is space under each goal in your Life List Planner to write down what you have learned about yourself and how you may have grown or changed from the experience.

This step can be expressed hand in hand with the next step, **Step 5: Gratitude**.

The Great Ski Adventure

Growth and lessons

1. Most of the greatest achievements in my life have occurred on the other side of fear. This is very true of skiing. I want to live my life in such a way that I embrace the fear and push through it. I will never let fear or lack stop me from launching myself outside my comfort zone.

2. It was very easy for me to identify my resisting forces (MOMENT: Step 3). And if not for challenging myself to reflect on what it is that I most value in this world (MOMENT: Step 4), I might never have gone skiing at all. What I value most in this world is the antidote to everything in the Fear Bucket and the Lack Bucket, and it always will be.

3. It is important to exit a ski lift with grace the moment you crest the top of the slope, as opposed to mistiming your disembarkation, gaining significant air and falling like a sack of poo onto the ice and tearing a muscle in your shoulder.

4. It is possible to break your thumb, bloody your lip and go very much arse over tit all at once when being taken out on a ski slope by a small French child who was born with skis already attached to his feet and who dive bombs you from behind like a fucking mosquito.

5. Being super cold and full of adrenalin is a wonderful mask for pain.

6. I didn't know it was possible to feel such joy watching my daughter's joy at being so much better than me at something. It was glorious.

7. You can actually laugh so hard that you do in fact wee your pants.

8. You can actually laugh so hard that you cannot regain your footing (or skis) for 37 minutes.

(continued)

9. It is possible to go down the scary runs completely on your bottom with your skis in the air so as to avoid dying. It is embarrassing but certainly doable.

10. Nice men controlling the ski lift will stop the lift to allow you to get on the lift at the top of the mountain and catch the lift down to the bottom of the mountain, completely against the flow of traffic, so that you don't die.

11. I am not ever going to go skiing again, ever. But you know what—I don't need to. I've already done it once. Tick.

12. Maybe there is an element of bravery in what I have done and what I am trying to do with my Life List, but mostly I think it's about a desperate desire to live my best life.

MOMENT

1. Set Your Intention
2. Pick a Goal
3. Identify Your Resisting Forces
4. Identify What You Most Value
5. Lock in a Deadline for the Goal

1. Mind Map the Goal
2. Lock in Deadlines for Each Action
3. Find Your Cheer Squad
4. Reframe Your Goal
5. Take a Step

MOMENTum

MOMENTous

1. Do It!
2. Celebrate
3. Share with the Squad
4. Acknowledge Your Growth and Lessons
5. **Express Your Gratitude**

5 Express Your Gratitude

Expressing gratitude is a daily habit I adopted soon after Dan became sick. It is not lost on me that it took his devastating diagnosis to prompt me to take the simple act of saying thank you for all of my blessings.

The simple joy of expressing gratitude

Each night when I lie in bed (one of my most favourite places in the world in any event) I spend five minutes reflecting on my day and expressing everything I am grateful for. On the 'good days' the list is long and self-affirming. On the 'bad days', while the list might be short, the act of expressing gratitude is a very powerful reminder that I am well, healthy, and loved by my family, and it never fails to refocus me and help me reframe my definition of what a 'bad day' actually means.

I am grateful that I created my Life List. I am grateful that I shared it with the world. I am grateful that it has provided the public accountability I needed to get out of bed and take back control of my life on my own terms. I am grateful for the support I have received for my Life List and my determination to master every moment to live an audacious life.

The research is very clear on gratitude—benefits include having a more positive frame of mind, greater self-confidence, feeling more alive, experiencing better sleep, stronger mental health and greater resilience.

I can personally attest to experiencing these benefits. I have achieved a significantly higher state of happiness through creating my Life List with the intention to live life on my own terms; the actual goals I have now had the joy of designing and doing; and the active gratitude I practise every day for being able to live a life by design.

It is for these reasons that I have built expressing gratitude as the final step of The Master Every Moment Framework—it is supremely powerful to actively cultivate an expression of thanks into our Life List on a regular and consistent basis.

Gratitude means showing appreciation for the amazing things in your life that bring you meaning, joy and purpose.

Gratitude means showing appreciation for the small things that you might sometimes take for granted.

Gratitude means acknowledging past regrets and reframing them to extract the learnings, knowing that you can draw on these experiences to live a better life.

Gratitude means appreciating what you have.

Gratitude means being thankful for what you have let go of.

Gratitude means appreciating what you have achieved.

Gratitude means appreciating what you can give to others.

In **Step 5: Express Your Gratitude**, after you complete each goal update your Life List to include what you are grateful for. The act of writing this down is important—not only will it help you with the process of self-reflection, but it will also create a permanent record that you can return to. Later, just reading this record will in itself lift your mood—allowing you to relive the experience and how it made you feel at the time.

List at least three things that you are grateful for in the experience.

Share what you are grateful for with your cheer squad—it will help you reflect more deeply on your experience.

There is space in your Life List Planner under each goal to record your gratitude.

The Great Ski Adventure

Gratitude

- I am grateful that my daughter wanted to spend time with me on what was a first for me.

- I am grateful that I got to experience skiing.

- I am grateful that I will never have to go skiing ever again.

- I am grateful that turning 50, losing my mum, losing Dan, facing the fact that my kids are breaking up with me and everything else that I have experienced over the last five years have led me to a place where I am very determined to make every single day count.

- I am grateful that I have my health.

- I am grateful that I have worked hard, that I am cashed up and that I am a 50ish woman with no more fucks to give.

- I am grateful that I get to master every moment to live an audacious life.

Never forget that every single MOMENTous change in your life starts with one small step—from now on, I want you to call this step a 'MOMENT'.

When you focus on and embrace each separate MOMENT and add another step and then another and then another, you create MOMEN-Tum.

It's time

And once you have MOMENTum, you are literally unstoppable as you create a life that is MOMENTous.

For me, it took but a moment to decide to embrace life and go skiing for the first time. It was just a moment in time, but it was life changing.

And so, my challenge to you is this: it's time to master every moment and live an audacious life.

Life is simply too short to do otherwise.

Section IV

My Life List

I want to share with you my current Life List. It is a constant work in progress and will continue to change and evolve as I continue to change and evolve.

My original Life List was a random set of things I wanted to do, experience or change. My current Life List is set out here in Section IV as an A–Z of how I will live life on my terms. Your Life List can be of any length and ordered any which way you like.

Like mine, your Life List will be a work in progress that will evolve as you do, and which you will add to or change as inspiration strikes.

I also have included goals in my Life List in different stages of development so that you can see how you might also work up your own Life List. For example, you will see that some of my goals are:

- just jotted down ideas at this stage—inspiration has struck and I have noted the goal down so as not to lose it

- partially worked up because I have started investing the time to think about what the goal looks and feels like

- fully worked up and ready to go with a deadline locked in

- completed and I have recorded how it turned out in the form of a journal entry including each step of The Master Every Moment Framework (except mind mapping).

I wanted to share my workings with you in this way so that you can see that working on your own Life List is an active, wonderful, ongoing, iterative experience that will never be complete.

I hope that my Life List is a source of inspiration and helps you create your own Life List—keep me posted!

Kate x

A

Agenda

[time] Affluence

Active

Art

B

Business planning
and development

C

Contributing

Courage

Curiosity

Charging what I am worth

Checking for lumps

D

De-clutter

Dance

E

Empowering myself to live a
life by design

Enough

F

Finance

Focus

First Class

Friendships

Fitness

Forgiveness

Family vacations

G

Growing a community of
incredible women

Glorious goals

Giraffes

Grit

Growth and Learnings

Gratitude

H

Hiking

Harry Potter World

Henry VIII

Help

I

Immersion in Italy

J

January

Joy

Journey

K

Knowledge

Kate

Kids

L

Love

Life List

Learning

Laughing

M

Marathon

Moments

Massage

Motorbike licence

N

New products in my business

No

O

Opportunity

Opera

P

Practice

Pelvic floor

Q

Quality clothing

R

Relocate to Bali

Rest and Replenish

Release

Risks

Reflection

Renewal

S

Swim Every Day

Stop

Swearing

Stretch

Sex

T

Travel as a digital nomad

Tattoo

Tenacity

Tact

Trailblazer

TED talk

U

Unlock new experiences

Unplug

Unafraid

V

Valuing what I most value

Versatile

Vulnerability

W

Woo woo

Well travelled

Wild

X

X-ing off alcohol

Kisses

Xoompin

Y

Yes Quest

Z

Zero out my carbon footprint

ZZZZZ

Zest for life

The Life List template

GOAL

REFLECTION

_____

_____

_____

GOAL TYPE

_____

_____

CHAPTER   DEADLINE

RESISTING FORCES

_____

_____

_____

WHAT I MOST VALUE

_____

_____

_____

CHEER SQUAD

_____

_____

REFRAMED GOAL

_____

_____

_____

TAKE A STEP

1.

2.

3.

4.

5.

CELEBRATE

ACKNOWLEDGE YOUR GROWTH AND LEARNINGS

EXPRESS YOUR GRATITUDE

MIND MAP

A is for my Agenda

GOAL — *Keep my daily agenda simple, focused and strategic.*

REFLECTION

I love simplicity. I love being time affluent. I love designing and living my perfect life. It makes sense to establish some basic habits for each day. And at the end of each day I can reflect on the fact that, if nothing else, I achieved the basics and I feel great about that.

GOAL TYPE

Go Small Goal

CHAPTER	*Health & Wellbeing, Lifestyle & Environment*	DEADLINE	*Immediate*

RESISTING FORCES

Lack of discipline.

WHAT I MOST VALUE

1. My time: it's precious and I am not prepared to waste it.

2. My family: the more disciplined I am with my daily agenda the more time I will have to be present for my family.

3. My business: the more disciplined I am with my daily agenda the more focused time I will have for my business — quality over quantity.

4. My health and wellbeing: the more disciplined I am with my daily agenda the more time I will have for exercise, reading, exploring, implementing my other goals and generally living my best life.

CHEER SQUAD

Just me for this one.

REFRAMED GOAL

I will keep my daily agenda simple with my top 10 daily experiences:

- *Swim every morning with my sisters*
- *Work on my high-value tasks from 8.30 am to 1 pm*
- *Batch everything*
- *Get it out of my head and onto paper – my brain is for strategising not for storage*
- *Be responsive, not reactive*
- *Deadline everything*
- *Invest my time in systemising what can be systemised*
- *Walk every afternoon*
- *Sit with my dad in the sun*
- *Check in with my kids.*

TAKE A STEP

1. Reflect on a typical morning.

2. Map it.

3. What things do I love doing that also set me up for success?

4.

5.

CELEBRATE

Not a Go Big Goal, but an impactful and important one – I get to enjoy and celebrate every afternoon as I sit with my dad, or exercise, or spend time with my kids, or plan my next big goal.

ACKNOWLEDGE YOUR GROWTH AND LEARNINGS

1. I have been batching my time for a long time, so the habit is already instilled. But this is an enhancement on the way I used to work because I am not over filling my daily agenda.

2. I love the simplicity.

EXPRESS YOUR GRATITUDE

1. I am grateful that I am so focused on where I invest my time.

2. I am grateful that I have worked hard to design and implement productivity strategies that ensure I am time affluent.

3. I am grateful for the routine; there is a comfort that comes from routine.

4. I am grateful that setting the basics up well has allowed me to move to a three-day work week.

A is for [time] Affluence

I have time in abundance.

A is for Active

Engaging in physical activities every day.

A is for Art

Visiting magnificent art collections around the world.

B is for Business planning and development

GOAL	To strategically and systematically focus on business planning and development.

REFLECTION

When you own a small business you need to hustle. Forever. It doesn't matter how successful you are this week or this year. You still need to hustle. There will be times or periods where your business is booming and growing organically and the work just seeks you out and it is easy and effortless and magical and... so, so dangerous.

I found myself in that place last year. Over a period of a few years my business had been booming. I had more than enough work and it was good work. My clients were fantastic, the work was stimulating and varied and I didn't need to do a thing to bring it in. It came knocking. And it was brilliant.

And I'll admit it — I got lazy, or complacent, or both probably. I took my eye off the business development ball because the work was simply there.

Fast forward to a space in my calendar where there were a few weeks that were quite literally empty and I was filled with a creeping sense of unease. I scheduled a call with my business coach and the conversation went something (or exactly) like this:

Coach: How are you, Kate?

Me: Well, I'm a bit flat actually. I don't really have a lot of work on.

Coach: Okay. What have you been doing over the last six months in terms of business development and to seed the market?

Me: Nothing. Okay. Yep. I see. Oh, fuck off. I get it.

I did actually tell my coach to fuck off. But he knows I love him and that I meant it in the nicest possible way. The fact is, I hadn't really done very much at all for business development and I had not sewn one little seed for new business for quite some time. The annoying thing is that this is not rocket science. My coach simply took me into the room of mirrors and reminded me to have a good hard look at myself. And it hurt.

That is why this one makes my Life List — because I love my business, I am good at what I do, but I genuinely need to take my own advice here — I can't sit back and wait for opportunities to come and fall into my lap. If I want it I have to create it for myself. Forever.

Life by design, baby.

GOAL TYPE

Go Small Goal (while it's a lot of work, it's not rocket science and nor does it tick my four goal rules, and so I am not classifying it as a Go Big Goal)

CHAPTER	Wealth, Growth, Lifestyle & Environment	DEADLINE	October annually

RESISTING FORCES

I hate the thought, and the act, of 'sales'. It genuinely makes my skin crawl. I would rather poke my eye out with a blunt stick than make a 'sales call'.

WHAT I MOST VALUE

1. My business: funnily enough, if I do not actively undertake business development and make the sales, then business can and will dry up.

2. My work and helping people: I love my clients and I love having an impact on their lives. I love it. I love it so much more than I hate the concept of 'selling'. If I share my content and write books and seed the market and put myself out there more and pick up the phone and make the calls and have the meetings and go for the coffees and write the emails — then bottom line, I can have an impact on more people. And helping people and making a difference in their lives by helping them get their time back and to set their goals or write their Life List and curate their perfect life is way more important to me than the creeping feeling of unease I experience when I think about 'sales'.

3. *My life by design: I love my life. I love my work. It is my drug of choice and it makes me feel fulfilled and joyful and energised and proud and I can't do any of that unless I engage in good solid business development.*

Okay. Good. Once again identifying what I most value has completely put shade on my Resisting Forces.

CHEER SQUAD

My business accountability girls (there are four of us and we meet regularly to keep each other on track).

REFRAMED GOAL

Each October I will work with my business accountability girls (you know who you are, my angels) to plan the following year. My business plan will be segmented with monthly deliverables and will include tasks such as:

- *revisiting my client avatars*
- *identifying which products to focus on, which products to retire and which new product(s) to develop*
- *clarifying my key messages*
- *identifying what updates are required for my website and business collateral*
- *identifying target partners*
- *developing targets for each product*
- *building my schedule for social media campaigns*
- *building my schedule for business development so that I am regularly seeding the market.*

I will track and measure against targets to help direct my focus. Every single task will have a deadline. I will identify what I can outsource so that I focus my time and effort on what I am best at.

TAKE A STEP

1. *Set my intention.*

2. *Lock deadlines into my calendar.*

3. *Create templates.*

4.

5.

CELEBRATE

While this is not a Go Big Goal, it does require a lot of planning and focus. I will celebrate each new client and every book sale and never take being in business for granted.

ACKNOWLEDGE YOUR GROWTH AND LEARNINGS

Discipline is king.

EXPRESS YOUR GRATITUDE

1. I am grateful that I have invested in a business coach who is prepared to hold me to account.

2. I am grateful that I have invested time and energy and love into developing a group of successful business accountability women who keep me focused and grounded. As individuals we are dynamic and driven women, but as a group of four we are truly invincible. I trust these women implicitly — I trust them with the intimate details of my business and I trust them to always tell me with complete honesty what will and what won't work. We have each other's backs and we always give and receive each other's truth.

3. I am grateful as I write this that I needed a kick up the butt to get planning for next year.

4. I am grateful that for our most recent October planning session, my business accountability buddies and I spent four days planning for our businesses as we hiked The 3 Capes in Tasmania. Combining hiking and being out in nature with business strategy is a no brainer. We had a lot of time together to discuss each of our unique businesses, we had a lot of time in our own heads to reflect and develop strategy and to build a vision for next year, and we had a lot of time each afternoon to sit and write it all up. It is exciting and stimulating and exactly what it needs to be — four clear days out of the office and amongst the trees to create a business plan that will keep me focused, curious, energised, pushing to do better and be better, and to deliver amazing results for my clients.

C is for Contributing

GOAL	To ensure that I contribute to and share my knowledge with others in business in the most effective and impactful way.

REFLECTION

I have always contributed my knowledge and expertise to others and I will continue to do so. But I want to contribute in a more deliberate rather than an ad hoc way. I want to determine exactly how and where I am going to donate my time, knowledge and money.

GOAL TYPE

Go Small Goal

CHAPTER	Giving	DEADLINE	Develop my Contribution Policy by January 2023

RESISTING FORCES

Lack of discipline.

WHAT I MOST VALUE

1. Helping others and making a genuine difference in people's personal and business lives.

2. Being organised and systematic in how I approach things.

3. Charities and causes that involve the education and health of girls and women.

CHEER SQUAD

The charities and causes that I support.

REFRAMED GOAL

It is January 2023 and I have developed a new Contribution Policy that articulates exactly how and where I share my knowledge and experience and my most valuable resource — my time — to causes that matter to me. I will focus on:

- charities and organisations that actively work to improve the health and education of girls and women
- advising start-ups to ensure they thrive and succeed
- mentoring other business owners
- giving back to my community.

TAKE A STEP

1. List all of the organisations/people where I currently donate my time, knowledge and money.

2. Reach out to them to formalise relationships and to ascertain exactly what they most need from me — how can I help them most?

3. Draft my Contribution Policy.

4.

5.

CELEBRATE

Not a Go Big Goal, just a 'get it done and feel better for having done so' kind of goal.

ACKNOWLEDGE YOUR GROWTH AND LEARNINGS

1. It isn't enough to want to contribute. Having a process and deadlines will turn this from a want into a discipline.

EXPRESS YOUR GRATITUDE

1. I am grateful that I have knowledge of value to share with causes that I value.

2. I am grateful that these causes have chosen to work with me.

3. It feels wonderful helping them.

C is for Courage

and not being afraid to be me and all of the wonderful, crazy, intense, quiet, funny, loud, often introverted, sometimes extroverted, candid, kind, loyal and alarming amazingness that entails.

C is for Curiosity

and for being ever so.

C is for Charging what I am worth

or charging nothing at all and having the courage to do both.

C is for Checking for lumps

and annual health check-ups, mammograms, pap smears, bowel tests, blood tests and everything else I need to do to make sure my kids get to spend a lot more time with me.

D is for Declutter

I will declutter and I will not accumulate.

The bin hire man was already in transit when I rang him and asked if I could have a bigger bin. I had underestimated just how much shit I had to throw out and, god bless him, he happily returned to the depot, unloaded the medium-sized bin, uploaded the supersized ginormous bin and headed back to my house.

After Dan and I separated, it was important for me to keep the kids in the family house to provide them with some sense of normalcy. A year later, when we were going through our financial settlement, we put the house on the market without luck. The market was in decline, the house was in the upper end of the housing market and apparently buyers were limited and acting with caution and the whole thing was a bloody nightmare. The one and only offer we received in two years was hundreds of thousands of dollars below what we were prepared to sell the house for.

I knew that if I could just hang on to the house long enough the market would eventually turn. In the end I bought Dan out of the property because so much of my future financial security was tied up in that place.

And this is the bit that utterly shits me to death. It was impossible for me — as a single mum with her own business — to get a mortgage. None of the major lenders would go near me. None of the minor lenders would go near me. Even though I had a lot of equity in the home and my business was experiencing significant year on year growth, bottom line for the banks was that I was a single mum and small business owner and the risk was far too great.

As women after separation there are so many odds stacked against us and I just applaud each and every one of us for prioritising our kids, turning up every single day and doing our absolute best in the face of such entrenched and institutionalised discrimination.

Eventually, my mortgage broker managed to find a loan at an interest rate above the residential market rate — which allowed me to buy Dan out of the house and to keep my kids in their family home.

I stayed in that house and paid that enormous mortgage on my own for another two years and it was financially exhausting.

During that time the house remained on the market and a total of three couples looked at it. The repayments were terrifying and I had no prospects of refinancing at any stage as I was still a single mum and still a small business owner. But I backed myself. I had so much faith that the market would turn — I just needed to hang on until it did.

It was spooky how the house eventually sold.

Dan was incredibly sick in hospital and in the last days of his life. We were in and out of the hospital every day and it was emotionally and physically an incredibly taxing time. Two days before Dan died I received a call from the real estate agent. He had a couple who wanted to look at the house — could he bring them through that week? Obviously that was a clear no. I explained our circumstances and he was wonderful and respectful and kind and that was that.

A week after Dan died, and I think the day or so before the funeral, the agent rang again. He was very apologetic, but the couple were super keen to see the house and would it be at all possible to get them through? He promised it would be quick, that I didn't need to tidy or clean or present the house and garden in any way at all even though the place was a shambles. The grass in the garden was thigh high. There were vases of flowers acknowledging Dan's passing on every available surface, and hampers of food sitting in the kitchen. There were clothes on the floor, washing in the basket, dog hair everywhere. Beds unmade. It was just awful.

Looking back now I cannot believe I said yes to that inspection. I was in shock and grieving and exhausted and overwhelmed and I think I just said yes because I was in such a state of fatigue where it was simply too hard to say no.

But after I said yes, I got angry. Mostly with myself. What on earth was I even thinking to entertain an inspection of our home the week of Dan's funeral?

And so when the agent arrived — a lovely, lovely man who is simply the best real estate agent I know — I wasn't in the mood to take any prisoners and I laid down the law: They have 15 minutes to view the house. I am not going to entertain any offer unless it is outrageously huge. Plus, I want a six-month settlement because my daughter is doing her final year of school and my kids have just lost their dad and there is no way I am going to fuck them up any more by moving out of our family house in 30 days.

Poor man.

My daughter and I left the house in complete disarray and took the dogs to the dog park and waited for the call 15 minutes later to tell us we could come home and that the couple were not interested. But the call didn't come.

Forty minutes later the agent called and we had an offer. It was outrageously huge. They were happy to settle in six months. They wanted to sign a contract the same day.

It was incredibly cathartic decluttering that house. The kids and I treated it like our own private smash room — taking sledgehammers to anything and everything prior to depositing it in that ginormous bin. We smashed the fridge because it was too big to move to the new house, we smashed the old TV, desks, chairs, tables, wardrobes. You name it. If it was big enough to smash, it was smashed. Talk about closure. The neighbours must have been terrified. It was glorious.

Decluttering is something I continue to be addicted to — which is why it makes my Life List.

GOAL TYPE

Go Small Goal

CHAPTER	Lifestyle & Environment	DEADLINE	Ongoing — actively embrace a good declutter

RESISTING FORCES

Fear of upsetting my kids by throwing things out.

WHAT I MOST VALUE

1. My kids. This one was simple — I got them involved in the declutter, nothing got thrown out without their okay and once they found the sledgehammers and realised they could smash anything that was in the potential chuck out pile it was a done deal.

2. A peaceful, minimalist environment that feels beautiful and soothing to live in.

3. A desire not to acquire (simply to later throw out).

CHEER SQUAD

The kids.

REFRAMED GOAL

I actively live with a state of mind that I will not acquire anything at all unless absolutely necessary. I have downsized where we live which means that I have also downsized our mass of possessions. This is a work in progress and sometimes things pop up and I wonder where on earth they came from. There are things in the garage that I did not even know we owned. Have we always had this useless thing? Where possible I recycle and I have donated hundreds of books to Goodwill. I have donated clothes and useful household items. If I no longer need something I do not hold on to it. I have lost a great deal of sentimentality over possessions.

TAKE A STEP

1. *Research bin hire — try and find local.*

2. *Lock into my calendar.*

3. *Lock into kids' calendars to make sure they are free to help me.*

4. *Find sledgehammers.*

5.

CELEBRATE

With a sledgehammer!

ACKNOWLEDGE YOUR GROWTH AND LEARNINGS

1. *I now realise that nothing gives me more pleasure than throwing crap out. I am freely letting go of possessions that no longer bring me joy. I am going to do more of it and I am going to double down by not accumulating 'stuff' in the first place. From now on, I am going to spend money on experiences not things.*

2. *I look back on that period of my life and I sometimes wonder how we made it through — with love and support and hope.*

EXPRESS YOUR GRATITUDE

1. *I am grateful that I had the courage and the resourcefulness to hold on to the family house until the market turned and I received a great offer.*

2. *I am grateful that such an awful period of my life is in the past.*

3. *I am grateful that I sold that house and that my kids and I could start afresh.*

4. *I am grateful to be living in a smaller house.*

5. *I am grateful that I have fewer possessions.*

D is for Dance

I will dance to my own set of rules — with absolute abandon. I simply do not care who is watching or judging or rolling their eyes at the wild chick on the dance floor. Because life's too short.

E is for Empowering myself to live a life by design

GOAL	I am passionate about empowering myself (and others — see 'I is for Inspiring the women') to create their own Life List and to live a life by design. I am passionate about sharing the message that it really is okay and actually quite wonderful to be a little selfish.

REFLECTION

Creating my own Life List has been a passion project. I am so excited to be my age, to have my layers of wisdom and wrinkles, to have the time, space, money and momentum to live a life by design.

GOAL TYPE

Go Big Goal

CHAPTER	Health & Wellbeing, Wealth, Adventure, Growth, Giving, Relationships, Lifestyle & Environment	DEADLINE	Now

RESISTING FORCES

1. Fear of failure.

2. Fear of people thinking I am selfish.

3. Fear of putting myself and my personal story out there — fear of exposure.

4. Fear of rejection.

5. Fear of polarising people.

WHAT I MOST VALUE

1. Living a brilliant life.

2. My kids and being a great role model.

3. My clients and a community of women who inspire me and who I want to inspire back.

4. My truth and owning it.

5. Helping others — hopefully my ongoing Life List journey and my story will resonate and help other women realise that they aren't alone, that it is okay to share your truth, that it is okay to feel how we are feeling and that it is okay to finally be a little more selfish or at least a little less selfless.

CHEER SQUAD

You.

REFRAMED GOAL

I am actively living out my Life List with excitement, vigour and joy. I have a great mix of Go Big Goals, Go Small Goals and Go Now Goals. I tackle a minimum of one Go Big Goal every year and I continue to write about and share my journey in my Life List blog (www.katechristie.com.au). I have empowered myself to live a life by design: no-one else is going to do it for me! I am excited and energised by the fact that I get to help other women from all around the world to live an empowered life by design. A life where they too can master every moment and live an audacious life.

TAKE A STEP

1. Create my Life List.

2. Select my goals.

3. Lock in my deadlines.

4.

5.

CELEBRATE

Writing The Life List has been a celebration in surviving and thriving after the hurdles thrown at me over the last five to six years. I celebrate every day that I have my kids, my dad and my sisters, my business, my health and my friends. Life is good.

ACKNOWLEDGE YOUR GROWTH AND LEARNINGS

1. I am a strong, resilient, confident woman who, when I set my mind to something, will always deliver.

2. I have a wonderful life, one that I get to design.

3. Life is way too short and I am determined to live it audaciously and exactly on my terms.

4. My determination to empower myself and other women to live their best life will not and does not appeal to everyone, and that's okay.

EXPRESS YOUR GRATITUDE

1. I am grateful for my grit, my hustle and my GSD ('Getting Shit Done') attitude to life.

2. I am grateful that you decided to come on this journey with me.

3. I am forever grateful for my life by design.

E is for Enough

and knowing when enough is enough.

F is for Finance

GOAL	Completely understand my financial position.
REFLECTION	

Within days of Dan telling me he wanted to leave our marriage I had a business meeting at one of the big banks to pitch for a project for my business. I was greeted by a lovely woman who led me to a conference room with breathtaking views across Melbourne and glass walls on all four sides.

And as we exchanged pleasantries and I commented on the view, she asked me possibly the most innocuous question of all time — 'How are you?'

And I burst into tears.

I was mortified — I was a blubbering stuttering mess. She was amazing. She rose from her chair, passed me a box of tissues and then lowered the blinds on each of those gaping glass walls to protect me from being exposed.

My pain and fear and vulnerability were so close to the surface that one simple, kind question about how I was doing completely disarmed me, and I lost it. I told her what had happened but I honestly don't remember much of the conversation. The one thing I do remember saying, however, and which has stayed with me since, was this: 'I don't even know how to open a bank account.'

That day I changed banks and for the first time since I was 23 years old I took responsibility for my own finances.

That wonderful woman is now one of my dearest friends. Her compassion, care, and selflessness on that day are her beautiful traits that I see from her every single time we catch up. It is just who she is. That meeting happened for a reason — it was embarrassing but it was also a gift. It changed everything.

In marriage and in partnerships there is a division of labour and responsibilities and we often play to our strengths. Finance was never a strength or an interest of mine. I completely absolved myself of the responsibility of our finances and left this to my husband. We always had joint bank accounts and investments and although he tried again and again, with great patience, to explain and involve me in our finances, I simply wasn't interested. We both had very good incomes, we lived well, there was never anything we couldn't have if we really wanted it, and so money was something I didn't really need to think or worry about.

After we separated I realised how brazen I had been. How much my indifference could have cost me if Dan wasn't a good and fair person. I had absolutely no idea how much money we had, where it was, how much the mortgage repayments were, how our finances and investments were structured, how much we had contributed to his superannuation in lieu of mine, how much we paid for his life insurance and income protection and not mine, how the beach house was bundled into a mortgage with our residence, how much the bills were and when they needed to be paid...And that was just our personal finances. On top of that I had never taken one iota of interest in my business finances beyond sending invoices, ensuring they were paid and then providing everything to my accountant at the end of the financial year. I just didn't care.

I am still furious with myself for my indifference. For my ignorance.

But with the patience and help of some amazing women — my banker (now a best friend) and my accountant (now a best friend) — I crawled out of that hole and am increasingly becoming financially literate. It is a work in progress.

This one makes my Life List because it is a reminder to me and to you that we simply don't know what challenges life is going to throw our way. It is critical to be financially present in your life.

GOAL TYPE

Go Big Goal (it's big because I have found the learning curve to be steep and challenging)

CHAPTER		DEADLINE	
	Wealth, Growth		Ongoing

RESISTING FORCES

1. Lack of knowledge — my internal script had always been one of I am not good at maths and I don't understand numbers.

2. Fear of having to close my business and go back into the corporate workforce.

WHAT I MOST VALUE

1. My kids and providing them with a stable life and future.

2. My kids and having the time and flexibility to set my own working hours around their needs.

3. My independence.

4. My business.

5. My clients and my work.

CHEER SQUAD

The women who have empowered me to know my numbers.

REFRAMED GOAL

I am actively engaged in understanding my financial position and I am 100 per cent financially literate. I regularly attend workshops and online tutorials to deepen my financial acumen. I invest in financial advice for myself and for my business. I have a financial plan for my personal wealth and I meet quarterly with my financial advisor to review my investments and my self-managed super fund. I meet every six months with my accountants to discuss my business finances and to plan for the next six months. Each year I make the maximum superannuation contributions. I know how to read my P&L and I check it three times a week and actively manage my expenses and income. I have a family budget and record all expenditure to allow me to forward plan. I understand my financial situation at all times. I have a plan for retirement. I don't pretend to understand something if I don't — I keep asking questions until I get it.

TAKE A STEP

1. Be brave enough to let my guard down and admit what I don't know.

2. Find experts to help me.

3. Batch blocks of time into my calendar for my financial education.

4. Lock in deadlines every month to stay on top of this.

5.

CELEBRATE

There are various layers of celebration here — including the ongoing friendships with my wonderful banking girlfriend and my beautiful accountant. More importantly, I actively campaign my friends and business colleagues and clients to prioritise their financial literacy, which is really important to me. I have a huge sense of relief and satisfaction that I now have this under control.

ACKNOWLEDGE YOUR GROWTH AND LEARNINGS

Knowledge is king.

EXPRESS YOUR GRATITUDE

1. I am grateful for the wonderful financially literate women in my life.

2. I am grateful to Dan for always taking care of our finances and for his patience in trying to educate me.

3. I am grateful that I have finally taken the time to educate myself financially.

4. I am grateful that I can read a P&L.

5. I am grateful that I have financial security.

6. I am grateful that I have prioritised the resources to invest in experts to help me financially plan for my future.

7. I am grateful that I can keep learning.

F is for Focus

I will focus on what makes me happy.

I will focus on my mental health.

I will focus on my physical health.

F is for Fly First Class

I will fly first class — even if it is just once.

F is for Friendships

I will cherish them and nourish them, not neglect them as I have sometimes done in the past. I will not spread myself too thin.

F is for Fitness

As a 50ish woman, it's important to be fit, healthy, active and have good strong muscles and bones.

F is for Forgiveness

I will readily forgive. Not because you didn't hurt me, not because I am a good person, not because I am grateful for the lessons, not because you deserve my forgiveness, not because I want to be liked by you, and not because I'm worried about karma — just because I have no more fucks to give and I do not want to waste my time giving you any more real-estate in my brain.

F is for Family vacations

and continuing to insist on having them regardless of how old the kids are because I love holidaying with my kids.

G is for Growing a community of incredible women

To coincide with the launch of this book I will grow a community of incredible, like-minded women who are hell bent on living their best lives.

REFLECTION

Time cannot be managed. Just like your money, your time is a limited and very precious resource that needs to be invested for the greatest possible return. A question I ask my clients and my audiences every single day is this – where do you really want to invest your time?

I have been sharing my expertise on how to find and harness 30-plus hours of lost time every month for over 10 years. More and more of my clients are regaining control of their time and they are looking for what is next – they want to learn how to use their time to design their perfect life. None of us wants to regain control of our time simply to fill those hours with more emails or another 20 loads of washing.

The concept of creating a Life List and curating a life by design has been playing out in my life personally over the last few years. I have reached the point where I have designed my perfect life and it is stupendous.

This book is all about inspiring others to do the same.

It is important to me to help as many women as possible to design their perfect life. In my discussions with women who are friends and clients, something that comes up time and again is the desire we all have to find a community of like-minded women to navigate this next chapter with. I want to help create and grow that community.

GOAL TYPE

Go Big Goal

CHAPTER	Health & Wellbeing, Growth, Giving, Relationships, Lifestyle & Environment	DEADLINE	April 2023 and onwards

RESISTING FORCES

1. Fear of failure.

2. What if no-one wants to play with me?

WHAT I MOST VALUE

1. My truth and owning it.

2. Helping others — hopefully my ongoing Life List journey and my story will resonate and help other women realise that they aren't alone, that it is okay to share your truth, that it is okay to feel how we are feeling and that it is okay to finally be a little more selfish or at least a little less selfless. The chance to help as many women as possible to realise that they can live a life by design. This is my driving force. It is so powerful that there simply is no resistance to this goal.

3. Continuing to live my best life.

4. Challenging myself and pushing myself out of my comfort zone: I know from my Life List that the fear of failure is a general recurring fear for me. But the more I work on my Life List and the more I push myself outside my comfort zone, the more I realise that I am dialling down the noise on this fear. Honestly — what is the worst thing that can happen? The women who resonate with my book and my style will join my community of like-minded women and the women who don't, won't. And that's okay.

CHEER SQUAD

My family, my accountability girls and most importantly — you.

REFRAMED GOAL

Let's go big with this! It is April 2023 and my book has hit the shelves with a bang! As part of a coordinated pre-launch marketing strategy I pre-sold more than 5000 copies which means that the book is an immediate bestseller on launch date. Within the first quarter I have sold 15 000 copies and by December 2023 I have sold 100 000 copies — which means that I have inspired 100 000 women to create their own Life List and to live a life by design. To live stupendously. By April 2023, my Life List Facebook group is set up and ready to go. I actively dive in and out of the page as hearing members' stories fills my cup and energises me so much more to keep helping them live their own Life by Design. By December 2023 the page has 10 000 members.

Yes! I also get to meet with you regularly on live calls, at events, and through my programs. Women reach out to me regularly by email and online to share their Life Lists and recent triumphs, and their momentum helps me maintain my own momentum. We are in this together.

TAKE A STEP

1. Map out the concept for the book.

2. Think chapters, flow and stories.

3. Create a word count chart and challenge: 1000 words a day!

4. Lock in my deadline.

5. Contact Wiley.

6. Mind Map out marketing campaign.

CELEBRATE

By continuing to live my best life. By celebrating with each of you as you live your best lives.

ACKNOWLEDGE YOUR GROWTH AND LEARNINGS

1. This is my fifth book and was by far the easiest to write; it literally poured out of me.

2. I set myself a target of 30 000 words in 30 days and I doubled this output. I clearly had a lot to say. Knowing that I am a morning person, I batched time into my calendar every day for six weeks to write each morning. I love it when I prove my time investment strategies to myself!

3. This is the first time I have written about the breakdown of my marriage and the death of Dan. I am a very private person, and so it was incredibly challenging to write about this topic and to find that fine line between sharing and oversharing. I made sure my kids were comfortable with what I have written and they were amazing — they gave their feedback and asked for some minor edits. It prompted a beautiful discussion with them and a lot of reflection and funny stories about their dad. It was cathartic for me to share this with you.

4. I hope very deeply that my sharing this story with you will help you live your very best life.

EXPRESS YOUR GRATITUDE

1. I am grateful to you.

2. I am grateful to my kids for their unconditional support.

G is for Glorious goals

Setting them and smashing them and then setting some more of them.

G is for Giraffes

and tigers, lions, wildebeest, gorillas, orangutans, sloths, toucans, polar bears, flamingos, narwhals, hippos, rhinos, elephants, puffins, penguins, zebras, pandas, lemurs and mandrills — and all of the animals I would love to see in their natural habitats.

G is for Grit

I am strong and determined and I dig deep.

G is for Growth and Learnings

I will always have a growth mindset and I will reflect on what I have learned, which is why I have built it into The Master Every Moment Framework.

G is for Gratitude

I will actively practise it every day, which is why I have built it into The Master Every Moment Framework.

H is for Hiking

GOAL	I will go on an incredibly challenging hiking adventure at least once a year.

REFLECTION

Over the course of my life, I have undertaken many day hikes, and a handful of multi-day hikes around the world including in Australia, America, England, Italy, Spain, France, Austria, Poland and Scotland. I want to hike more, get out in nature, unplug and continue to push myself to take on more challenging hikes.

In pursuit of living out my Life List, in 2022 I chose as my Go Big Goal to hike 130 km of the 223 km Larapinta Trail, which runs from Alice Springs along the spine of the West MacDonnell Ranges in Central Australia. The experience was without question a million times harder than I could possibly have imagined or prepared for — physically, emotionally and mentally. For mine, it was a cross between Survivor, SAS and The Hunger Games.

To be fair, the trek website did grade the hike as 'Epic' — which turned out to be code for really fucking hard. The website also contained other obvious giveaways, such as this little chestnut: 'The trek involves challenging to very challenging walking between 7 to 12 hours each day, across very rocky terrain and ridge lines, with steep ascents and descents.'

But here's the thing — just like experiencing childbirth, the more time that passes since a gruelling hike, the more value I seem to gain from the experience and the more inclined I am to go back for more. Go figure.

I call this 'latent enjoyment' — one of my hiking buddies calls it 'Type 2 Fun'.

GOAL TYPE

Go Big Goal

CHAPTER	Adventure, Lifestyle & Environment, Health & Wellbeing	DEADLINE	Every year

RESISTING FORCES

(for the Larapinta trek, and likely to be very similar resisting forces in future hikes)

1. Fear of getting hurt in the middle of nowhere and having to be airlifted out after spending a freezing cold night under a tinfoil blanket.

2. Fear of EOMB – a.k.a. early onset mud bum (it is an actual thing and pretty much means the accumulation of a little residue of poo every day because there are no showers…).

3. Fear of not being fit enough.

4. Fear of my feet/back/entire body breaking down.

5. Fear of snakes.

6. Fear of spiders.

7. Fear of getting dehydrated.

8. Fear of not being mentally strong enough.

9. Fear of not finishing the hike.

10. Fear of not being able to keep up with the group and being voted off the island on the first night.

WHAT I MOST VALUE

1. Challenging myself physically and mentally.

2. Experiencing beautiful and remote parts of the world.

3. Doing something that is just for me.

4. Writing about the experience and inspiring others to live a life by design.

5. Getting off the train every now and then. Just stopping.

CHEER SQUAD

My kids.

My dad.

My sisters.

My hiking buddies – honestly without them I don't know how I would complete each hike.

I will plan for and enjoy at least one new multi-day hike every year. I will mix up the locations, the length of the hike, the amount of weight I carry, the level of support provided by the trekking company, and the level of the challenge. Some hikes will be luxurious, some will be fully supported, some partially supported and some will involve going it alone with a hiking buddy or two, a map and a compass. Target locations include:

- *Australia:*
  - *The Larapinta (completed May 2022 — if you want to read more extensively about this six day epic hike, go to my website at www. katechristie.com.au for a full breakdown of the trip along with the incredible photos)*
  - *The 3 Capes (completed October 2022 — if you want to read more about this hike, go to my website at www.katechristie.com.au)*
  - *The Overland (completed November 2022 — for the photos, videos, the 'thunder snow', the blizzard, the mud and all of the glorious details of this epic Tasmanian trek, go to my website at www. katechristie.com.au.)*
  - *The Great Ocean Walk*
  - *Kakadu*
  - *Fraser Island*
  - *Cape to Cape WA*
  - *The Bungle Bungles*
- *South America:*
  - *The Inca Trail*
  - *Fitz Roy Trek*
  - *Orres Del Paine Circuit*
- *Nepal:*
  - *The Annapurna Circuit*
- *Greenland:*
  - *The Arctic Circle Trail*

- Europe:
  - Camino Primitivo, Camino de Santiago, Spain
  - Dolomite High Route, Italy
  - Lycian Way, Turkey
  - Iceland Trail, Iceland

TAKE A STEP

For the Larapinta Trail, and for any hike I do, these are the typical steps I take.

1. Research trekking companies who specialise in the hike.

2. Convince a hiking buddy to come with me because I am too scared to do it on my own.

3. Find dates that suit.

4. Lock it in.

5. Research gear and buy what I need.

6. Research first aid issues.

CELEBRATE

After finishing the Larapinta Trail I was physically spent for a good two weeks. My eyes and face puffed up like I had been stung by bees. I am seriously not at all sure what that was about. Immediately on falling over the threshold to the hotel room in Alice Springs I sat on the floor of the shower and scrubbed half the desert from my dirty skin, washed my hair and crawled from the bathroom to my very comfortable bed. We later enjoyed a glass of wine, an early dinner and fell into bed before sleeping for 10 hours straight.

ACKNOWLEDGE YOUR GROWTH AND LEARNINGS

1. The Larapinta trail is rocky. Very rocky. Pretty much 85 per cent of what you walk on, look at, sit on, scramble up, trip over and fall on is...rock. The rocks are spectacular and amongst the oldest on earth at 2000 million years old.

2. When I hike I fall over. Every single time.

3. Don't sleep under the stars unless you want mice to run across your face.

4. A trek rated 'epic' on its website is not for the faint hearted or chicks who are worried about falling over or for people hoping not to trip and die.

5. Shake your sleeping bag out every single night because spiders love to snuggle.

6. Don't squat over spinifex grass when you need to do a 'bush wee' — this stuff is not wispy grass, but spiky, hard-as-nails, arrow-tipped barbs that, if you get one imbedded in your bum cheek, hurt a bloody lot and are very hard to extract. Trust me on this one.

7. Commencing a hike at 1.30 am wearing a head torch and climbing a mountain for four hours in the dark is definitely worth it for the most stunningly spectacular sunrise on earth.

8. While I missed my kids, I didn't spend hours wondering if they were okay. I know they are smart, resourceful, resilient young adults and they can do very well indeed without me every now and then. And I can do very well indeed without them every now and then. It's time to step back, relinquish some control and let them work out stuff for themselves. We have had a few very hard years but we are all going to be okay. This will be good for them and for me.

9. Without question, this was the hardest physical, emotional, mental and spiritual challenge I have ever experienced. Seriously, skiing was a piece of cake compared to this. I didn't get voted off the island and I'm phenomenally proud of what I achieved.

10. Latent enjoyment (or Type 2 Fun) is a wonderful thing.

11. I know without a doubt that I can do absolutely anything — anything — that I set my mind to. I am powerful. I am strong. I really am.

12. Fixamol is better for blisters than bandaids.

13. It was supremely wonderful to take an extended break from the constant, incessant accessibility of mobile phones and laptops. I spent a good part of the week in my brain on my own and I have decided it's a pretty good place to hang out. And while I was reluctant to reconnect to wifi, the afternoon the hike ended the pull of making sure the kids were still alive and sharing with them the news that their mum is a hardcore SAS rockstar was too strong. I called home and revelled in their admiration and cried when they told me how proud they are of me.

14. I said goodbye to Dan as a brave man who lost his fight with cancer way too young. I miss him and that's okay. I promised him to continue to be the best possible mum to our kids.

15. And most importantly — it is very, very okay to prioritise myself and my needs and my Life List without any sense of guilt. I absolutely deserve to live an exceptional, stupendous, audacious life without limits — a life that is a little more selfish — and that's what I plan to do.

EXPRESS YOUR GRATITUDE

1. I am grateful for my health and while my left knee killed and I limped across the finish line, my back was completely fine.

2. I am grateful for my sense of humour because there was a lot about the Larapinta walk that wasn't fun.

3. I am grateful for making new friends amongst my fellow hikers and for deepening my friendship with my hiking buddy. I now regularly walk with one of my new hiking friends.

4. I am grateful to the trekking company we walked with and the two passionate, knowledgeable and talented guides who supported our hike.

5. I am grateful for new skills — like erecting a tent.

6. I am grateful that I did not get early onset mud bum or come face to face with a snake.

7. I am grateful that I did not give up and have a rest day, in the face of great temptation.

8. I am grateful to live in an extraordinarily old and beautiful country.

9. I am grateful to the Traditional Owners of this land for allowing us access to it.

10. I am grateful to have reignited my passion for hiking.

11. I am grateful for being mentally and physically stronger than I thought I was.

12. I am grateful to have the time, money and independence to live a stupendous, audacious life by design.

H is for Harry Potter World

I simply love Harry Potter and I want to go to Harry Potter World. Let me know if you want to come with me.

H is for Henry VIII

I am fascinated by this period of history. I love reading about it and I want to keep exploring it.

H is for Help

I will ask for it when I need it. I will give it even when it isn't asked for.

I is for Immersion in Italy

GOAL	*I will live in Italy and completely immerse myself in that magnificent culture.*

REFLECTION

I love Italy. When I was 22 I travelled extensively through Europe and I spent four weeks living and working in a youth hostel on Lake Como. My friend and I got to stay in an apartment in Menaggio and our job each day was to help serve breakfast and dinner and to wash a few loads of bed linen. That was it. For the other 10 hours of the day we got to hike the mountains, swim in the lake and the rivers, hitch hike into Switzerland and back for the day, mountain bike ride and eat gelato. It was delightful. Later, Dan and I holidayed together in Italy before we had kids and in 2011 we spent 11 weeks there as a family. I want to set myself up in an ancient little town somewhere and eat and play and learn Italian and have a simmering Italian love affair or two. Oh, and work. Of course. That's the whole idea—I will also work.

GOAL TYPE

Go Big Goal

CHAPTER	Health & Wellbeing, Adventure, Growth, Relationships, Lifestyle & Environment	DEADLINE	*2024/5?*

RESISTING FORCES

1. *Fear of failure.*

2. *Fear of people thinking I am selfish.*

3. *Fear of impacting my business.*

4. *Missing my kids and family.*

WHAT I MOST VALUE

1. *Living a brilliant life and not leaving anything on the table.*

2. *Curiosity, learning, experiencing different cultures.*

3. *Pasta.*

CHEER SQUAD

You.

REFRAMED GOAL

It is [2024/2025?] and I am able to have a real conversation in Italian. I have tried three times over the years to learn Italian and this time I did it. I am nowhere near fluent but I can get by quite nicely. I am living in a lovely little village in the countryside. I made friends with the local baker given the alarming amount of bread I buy and consume, who in turn introduced me to all of the locals. I have been welcomed with open arms into the operating rhythm of this beautiful place. I have made friends of all ages and I am surrounded by words, architecture, art, food and culture of such beauty that I feel as if I will never leave. Oh, and my kids are coming to visit next week and they convinced my dad to come too.

TAKE A STEP

1.

2.

3.

4.

5.

CELEBRATE

ACKNOWLEDGE YOUR GROWTH AND LEARNINGS

EXPRESS YOUR GRATITUDE

J is for January

GOAL	Choose a word for the year.

REFLECTION

Every January for at least the last five years I have declared one new word as the word that will inspire my direction and focus and energy for the year. The word I choose sets my intention for the whole year and whenever I find myself getting off track or losing focus or feeling flat, I remind myself of that word as it helps me cut through the noise.

GOAL TYPE

Go Small Goal

CHAPTER	Health & Wellbeing, Growth, Lifestyle & Environment	DEADLINE	January annually

RESISTING FORCES

None, it's fun.

WHAT I MOST VALUE

Autonomy and choice.

CHEER SQUAD

Everyone! I share my word every year. I would love for you to share yours with me too.

REFRAMED GOAL

It is January [year] and I have set my intention for the year with one word that grounds me and ensures I act consistently and with focus for the whole year. This year my word is...

TAKE A STEP

1. Set a deadline to coincide with my annual business planning to think about a word that best sums up how I want the following year to play out.

2. Often a word will just pop into my brain and I will know that it is THE word.

3. If this doesn't happen (which it generally does), work through some different options.

4. Shortlist the words.

5. Sit with the shortlist until one word stands out.

CELEBRATE

When I have the word locked in, share it with my business accountability girls.

ACKNOWLEDGE YOUR GROWTH AND LEARNINGS

1. In 2022 my word was 'Effortless' – the year, my work, my interactions with everyone around me, my dreams, my goals, my focus, my approach, writing this book – was all intended to be effortless. This didn't mean that my year was without effort or free of challenges, it just meant that my intention was that my year was not to be effortful. For me, it was a year of greater rest, recovery and reflection after five challenging years.

2. In previous years I have set my annual intention with words such as Growth, Consolidation, Hustle.

3. In 2023 my word is Expansion. Expansion of my personal life and growth, expansion of my relationships and continuing to discard any remaining baggage from the past, expansion of my business, expansion of my happiness, expansion of my horizons, expansion of my Life List. God that word feels good.

EXPRESS YOUR GRATITUDE

1. I am grateful for my autonomy and for having choice.

2. I am grateful that setting my intention this way each January actually works – there have been plenty of times when reminding myself of my word has brought me back on track.

J is for Joy

Experience joy often.

J is for the Journey

Enjoy the ride, lady.

K is for Knowledge

GOAL	To keep learning forever.

REFLECTION

There I was, in an Uber on the way back from a very big day out in Hobart with my girlfriend. This was way before the Yes Quest (see Y is for Yes) but it was certainly an eye opener into just how much you can fit into a day. We woke early and went for an autumn swim (and as Hobart is one of the few gateways to the Antarctic, let me tell you it was a new level of cold for me), followed by breakfast on the docks, a drive into the country for lunch at a winery followed by a sneaky afternoon nap and then the opening of an art exhibition, dancing to a street band at a hops festival, and then a drive back into town for a late dinner at a luxe restaurant with cocktails and wine before falling into the Uber.

My friends were giggling in the back seat about something ridiculous and reminiscing about the day. And me? Well, I was in the front seat talking to the Uber driver about his business model.

I love learning about people and their businesses or their jobs and their lives.

This one makes the Life List because I never want to lose sight of my thirst for knowledge. Curiosity didn't kill the cat. Curiosity helped her thrive and grow and curate her perfect life.

GOAL TYPE

Go Small Goal

CHAPTER	Growth	DEADLINE	Ongoing

RESISTING FORCES

Fatigue and sometimes being complacent.

WHAT I MOST VALUE

1. Being curious.

2. Establishing relationships with people.

3. Learning about new ideas, creating new opportunities, exploring and acquiring content.

4. Sharing my own knowledge.

5. Growth.

CHEER SQUAD

You.

REFRAMED GOAL

I will acquire, grow and share my knowledge. I have a business coach to maximise my business growth, to support me in pushing myself outside my comfort zone, to provide perspective and tools, and to challenge my thinking. I actively acquire knowledge by engaging in business programs, attending events, engaging in interesting conversations, and being consistently curious and well read. I generously share my knowledge with my clients, my community of incredible women, my accountability groups, the charities and organisations I support, the publications I write for, and the people I mentor. I am focused on personal growth and actively curious about spirituality, thinking differently, understanding other cultures and learning about other people and what makes them tick. I like to acquire knowledge.

TAKE A STEP

1. Ask questions.

2. Learn something new each day.

3. Listen more than you talk.

4. Surround yourself with wise people, beautiful books and learning opportunities.

5. Try something different, often.

CELEBRATE

By reflecting on what I have learnt and on sharing new knowledge with others.

ACKNOWLEDGE YOUR GROWTH AND LEARNINGS

This goal is self-fulfilling — I am learning every single day.

EXPRESS YOUR GRATITUDE

1. *I am truly grateful that I am a curious being.*

2. *I am grateful when people generously share their knowledge with me.*

3. *I am grateful that I am a voracious reader.*

K is for Kate

Of course! I am mastering every moment to live an audacious life.

K is for my Kids

Because they are the most important people in my life. This book is all about my Life List and how I want to design my best life, but my best life includes my kids and their happiness. I will always be there for them. I will always drop everything for them. I will always be in their orbit. But I know that they need me to be actively present so much less than they used to... which opens me up to a lot more of 'K is for Kate'.

L is for new Love

GOAL	*I would love to find new love. The love of my life sort of love. Not a beige fill a gap kind of love.*

REFLECTION

Thinking through my resisting forces below and then what it is that I most value and writing it down here has given me significant perspective. It has helped me realise that I am pretty damn happy as a single women with complete autonomy over my life. I get to decide everything for myself without the need to consult or compromise and that is very valuable to me.

I have built an amazing business and I am thriving professionally. I am financially secure and independent. I don't need a knight in shining armour to rescue me. I have already rescued myself.

I have a wonderful group of supportive, fun, intelligent and engaged group of family and friends in my life. I am not lonely.

It would definitely be wonderful and enriching to have breathtaking, mind-blowing, leg-shaking sex with someone, but let's be honest, I don't actually need to be in love for that to happen. I can also have exceptionally good sex with myself.

Sex and giving someone access to my body isn't the most valuable gift I have to give. My more precious gifts are free and unconditional access to my beautiful brain, my thoughts and feelings, my unwavering support and loyalty, my enthusiasm and passion, and to my feelings and observations. And to win that you must truly be special.

Articulating this makes me realise that while it would be very lovely to fall in love, it needs to be the right kind of love. I am simply not prepared to settle for any kind of love. I am not prepared to settle, full stop.

GOAL TYPE

Go Big Goal in that it will be big and wonderful and impactful when it happens. But also a Go Small Goal in that I do not plan to go looking for him at all; he will find me.

CHAPTER	Health & Wellbeing, Adventure, Giving, Relationships, Lifestyle & Environment	DEADLINE	There is no deadline.

RESISTING FORCES

Oh my god, where to start...

1. Fear of being rejected.

2. Fear of being hurt.

3. Fear of people knowing my business.

4. Fear of making a fool of myself.

5. Fear of being lonely.

6. Fear of being lied to.

7. Fear of being cheated on.

8. Fear of not being loved.

9. Fear of not being able to trust.

Seriously... I could keep going here, but I am assuming that this is enough to work with for now.

WHAT I MOST VALUE

1. I value my independence – which I recognise does not help with the above Resisting Forces but it does give me clarity and perspective about what I really want for my life. It does help me frame up exactly what it is I am looking for and exactly what it is I am not prepared to compromise on.

2. I value my autonomy – also good for helping me reframe.

3. *I value being valued – it would be wonderful to be that very special person for a very special person.*

4. *I value travel and experiences and adventure and it would be perfect to have a partner to share these experiences with.*

5. *I value my worth.*

6. *I value consistency and honesty and trust and respect and loyalty. I give these things and I require them in return.*

CHEER SQUAD

You.

REFRAMED GOAL

So, to be my new love, to be my partner and soul mate – here is who you are:

You are honest and trustworthy. You are wise, protective and compassionate. You make me laugh. You are driven, successful, independent and love time to yourself. You are family oriented and share similar values to me. You are passionate, tactile and when you take me in your arms I will feel secure and protected. You have taken the time to work through whatever shit you were carrying and you have lightened the load of your baggage. When you look at me and touch me I feel so desired that I am breathless. You are genuinely interested in my happiness – you value my opinion and trust me as your best friend and lover. You are ready to commit, to travel the world, to enjoy life on our terms and we can build a Partner Life List together. You are tall with broad shoulders and beautiful hands. You make me weak at the knees. You have this lovely little crinkle in the corner of your eyes when you look at me and smile. You are kind. You make me feel loved and valued. We support each other's dreams.

I so look forward to meeting you.

TAKE A STEP

CELEBRATE

ACKNOWLEDGE YOUR GROWTH AND LEARNINGS

EXPRESS YOUR GRATITUDE

L is for Life List

Done and ever growing and sprinkled with the audacious.

L is for Learning

I have a lot to learn. I want to learn how to:

- Surf — maybe I can do this in Bali?

- Skateboard — not tricks, just how to ride one

- Take great photos

- Use Instagram properly

- Use my CRM well enough so that I know exactly what to ask my VA to create

- Do a proper squat, I think I do something weird that makes my back hurt

- Program the TV

- Program the internet

- Stop over analysing

- Tell if someone is lying

- Spin a pen across my fingers — I don't even know how to describe this but it is very cool when I see people do it

- Touch type

- Whistle using my fingers

- Knit including how to cast the stitches

- Draw a nose that looks like a nose

- Read constellations

— Read tarot

— Take proper care of my skin with the right products

— Do a kick arse karate kick

— Dance the salsa

— Meditate properly

— Stretch properly

— Switch off

— Find my core and strengthen it

— Find my glutes and strengthen them

— Find my pelvic floor and engage it

— Maximise my gut health because a bloated gut seriously sucks

— Run efficiently

— Drive a truck

— Edit videos.

L is for Laughing

with a deep and joyful abandon every single day. I want to laugh until I wet my pants (... see 'P is for Pelvic Floor').

M is for Marathon

GOAL	Run a half marathon and then maybe even a full marathon.

REFLECTION

When I was in my early 40s I set myself a very loosey-goosey goal that I would run the Boston Marathon before I turned 50. I was quite fit at the time and doing a lot of running and it seemed like a good goal to have. But then the Resisting Forces reared up and planted a veritable forest of doubt in my brain — it was going to be too hard to plan, too far to travel, too far to run, it would cost a lot of money for a personal indulgence, I would need to take time off work, as would my husband, and we would need to pull the kids out of school, and it was too disruptive and...

And then life took over and it just didn't happen. And I regret it — I regret it enough that I am going to do something about it. Regret is a huge motivator — don't you think?

GOAL TYPE

Go Big Goal

CHAPTER	Health & Wellbeing, Adventure, Growth	DEADLINE	TBD 2024?

RESISTING FORCES

1. I am not anywhere near match fit.

2. It's scary thinking about running that far.

3. My pelvic floor ain't what she used to be — not since I pushed three gigantic babies out of my vagina 20 years ago.

4. Fear of hurting my back — it's generally a bit unstable and when it goes it isn't fun.

5. That's about it really — I can't say that time or money or permission or anything else is a Resisting Force for me any more. I don't have the luxury of those excuses getting in my way. Damn it.

WHAT I MOST VALUE

1. *Achieving something incredibly challenging — how wonderful and proud I will be of myself to achieve this long-held goal.*

2. *Pushing myself way outside my comfort zone.*

3. *My business — like all of my Go Big Goals, these sorts of experiences provide me with so much content to share.*

CHEER SQUAD

Ohhhh, just imagine having my kids at the finish line cheering me on!

REFRAMED GOAL

It is [date] and I am lining up at the start of the [location] Marathon and it is a stunning morning. I am nervous but excited and I have only done two nervy poos. I have been preparing for six months including lots of walking, hiking, personal training and of course running — I started off with a very slow 5 km and built this up over time.

I have been eating well — lots of protein and vegetables. I created a half marathon training plan and I stuck to it. I did a practice 10 km race a few weeks ago so that I could experience race day conditions (not that I am 'racing' but you know what I mean).

TAKE A STEP

CELEBRATE

ACKNOWLEDGE YOUR GROWTH AND LEARNINGS

EXPRESS YOUR GRATITUDE

M is for Moments

My favourite word in the world – M is for moments, and momentum and being momentous and for The Master Every Moment Framework and for making every single moment count.

M is for Massage

I will aim to enjoy a massage at least twice a month or maybe every week.

M is for Motorbike licence

I want to get this so that I can ride around Bali and be covered by travel insurance.

N is for New products in my business

| GOAL | I will consistently create new products in my business. |

REFLECTION

It's important to keep my business fresh and responsive to the needs of my clients by introducing a new product or service every year. It's important to my brain to keep things fresh and interesting so that I continue to love what I do and to grow.

GOAL TYPE

Go Big Goal

| CHAPTER | Wealth, Growth, Giving | DEADLINE | Designed in annual planning cycle (October) to be implemented in the first quarter of every year. |

RESISTING FORCES

1. Fear of failing — what if it doesn't sell; what if it doesn't work; what if you don't love it, what if something goes wrong, what if...?

2. Fear of pandemics — what if pandemic restrictions are reintroduced?

3. Fear of being judged — putting myself out there is a scary.

WHAT I MOST VALUE

1. Helping you: I am so driven to help as many women as I can. I love nothing more than the validation I get from hearing from you — my clients and readers — that I have in some way helped you design and live your own best life. I love to see you thrive. It is amazing.

2. *My business: my business is one of the things I value most. I grew my business from absolutely nothing and I am really proud of myself for what I have created and how I have gone about creating it. It was my focus and my lifeline in the hardest five years of my life. This is a chance to create a new product each year for my business, and that's exciting.*

3. *Growth and pushing myself outside my comfort zone. I am never truly happy unless I am challenging myself.*

Boom. See you later Resisting Forces.

CHEER SQUAD

My business accountability group, my coach, my family and you (given I have gone all public accountability on this).

REFRAMED GOAL

It is the final quarter of 2023 and I have just run my first Life List Retreat. I capped the retreat at eight to 10 women to ensure I could give my focus to each and every one of them. I was nervous but thrilled and excited when the retreat sold out within two months of announcing the dates. The retreat ran for a week and attendees used this time to create their own amazing Life List using the Life List Planner. They applied The Master Every Moment Framework to their Life List and they have prioritised and completely worked up their first Go Big Goal. They participated in a range of activities designed to enhance their growth, knowledge, health and wellbeing. They made new friends and have a tight accountability group and cheer squad. They loved the retreat. I loved the retreat. It will be the first of many.

It's February 2024 and I have just introduced my new product X...

TAKE A STEP

CELEBRATE

ACKNOWLEDGE YOUR GROWTH AND LEARNINGS

EXPRESS YOUR GRATITUDE

N is for saying No when I might otherwise have said yes

Say NO like a boss. I will say No more often. I will set boundaries that protect my time and my energy. I am getting better at this, but there is room for greater growth. Contrary to the Yes Quest which is all about saying Yes to things I would normally say No to, this one is about ensuring that I stop doing the things that do not bring me joy. Each time I say No to something I don't want to do, I get to replace it with a Yes to myself and something I do want to do.

O is for Opportunity

GOAL — *Be open to opportunity. Read the signs.*

REFLECTION

My Life List is all about setting my intentions for the life I want to live. But it is also so important to be open to, and available for, opportunities as they arise. This one is closely linked to the Yes Quest — I will be ready to jump when I see the chance.

GOAL TYPE

Go Now Goal

CHAPTER — *Growth, Adventure, Lifestyle & Environment*

DEADLINE — *Ongoing*

RESISTING FORCES

None.

WHAT I MOST VALUE

1. Having some fun.

2. Mixing things up a little.

CHEER SQUAD

Just me.

REFRAMED GOAL

In line with 'W is for Woo Woo', I actively look out for signs that might point me in the right direction in my life, or even in a different direction. Prior to creating my first Life List and more intentionally looking to design my life, I had been so single-minded in pursuing my goals one goal at a time that I think I may have missed some of the signposts along the way. I am going to pay better attention to the signs — it might open me up to a different path to follow altogether. I mean this in a very literal sense. It is not so much that I see a rainbow and think that new opportunities are around the corner. It's more that I will find actual street signs or posters or any form of written or spoken word that piques my interest and which I describe as beyond coincidence, and I will reflect on those signs and maybe change things up a little.

TAKE A STEP

1. Be ready...

CELEBRATE

By writing about it in my Life List blog (to follow my Life List journeys go to www.katechristie.com.au).

ACKNOWLEDGE YOUR GROWTH AND LEARNINGS

I started collecting 'signs' as a bit of fun, but it has become a bit of a compulsion and perhaps not just a matter of 'fun'. While some of the signs do make me laugh, others are thought-provoking and some have literally popped up in front of me as a message from the universe with such serendipity that it has prompted me to change tack, seize the opportunity or let something go because it is no longer serving me.

Here's a sample of some of the signs that have found me:

Hurry Slowly

You are given one sunset a day

Resist the urge to start with the biggest slide first — start small & build up your comfort level

In case of Tsunami go up the tower

Please do not feed the squirrels

Finish point of CLIMAX

Control Yourself

Note to self: Let shit go

Slide at your own risk

One moment please — rescue in progress

Skinny people are easier to kidnap — stay safe, eat a burger

Embrace the mystery

If your child is nervous go down the slide first so you can wait for them at the bottom

Stay connected

Sometimes what didn't work out for you really worked out for you

If you can't beat the fear — just do it scared

Disturbingly flourishing

EXPRESS YOUR GRATITUDE

1. I gratefully embrace being a little quirky.

2. I am grateful to be present enough to look for the signs.

O is for Opera

and going to the opera in Vienna and sitting in an exquisite opera box

P is for Practice

GOAL	Commit to a daily practice of improving myself.

REFLECTION

It is important to me to be self-aware, to continue to hone my skills and to make the time to improve on the areas or behaviours where I know I need to grow.

GOAL TYPE

Go Small Goal

CHAPTER	Health & Wellbeing, Growth, Lifestyle & Environment	DEADLINE	Ongoing

RESISTING FORCES

It doesn't necessarily have the allure or excitement of my other goals. It feels like more of a chore. It has a I need to do this as opposed to a I want to do this, feel about it (which is probably a good indication that it needs to be done...).

WHAT I MOST VALUE

1. Curiosity.

2. Growth.

3. Self-awareness.

CHEER SQUAD

Just me.

REFRAMED GOAL

I actively practise self-awareness and hone in on my areas of strength and my areas for growth.

In addition to continuing to focus on my strengths to make them more robust, I have identified five key areas of growth that I will focus on each day.

These five areas represent things I am okay at but could be much better at, things I am great at but with inconsistent application, or things I truly suck at and which I want to develop a solid, repeatable connection with:

- *Pursuing my passions*
- *Gratitude*
- *Positive self-talk*
- *Patience*
- *Perspective.*

TAKE A STEP

1. Jump into my calendar and batch in time to plan this out properly.

CELEBRATE

ACKNOWLEDGE YOUR GROWTH AND LEARNINGS

EXPRESS YOUR GRATITUDE

P is for Pelvic Floor

For god's sake, find it and work on it.

Q is for Quality Clothes

GOAL — Establish a clothing label with my sisters.

REFLECTION

I am finding it increasingly hard to find beautiful, quality clothes that make me look stylish, chic, stunning and which also feel comfortable. Everything I see seems to be fast fashion, ridiculously expensive, or targeted at 20-year-olds with very different bodies to mine.

What the hell is it with cropped jumpers? Or cropped anything for that matter?

My wonderfully creative sisters feel exactly the same way and because we love and adore each other and want to work together, we have decided to start our own clothing label. I mean, why not?

GOAL TYPE

Go Big Goal

CHAPTER	Wealth, Growth, Relationships, Lifestyle & Environment	DEADLINE	Late 2023

RESISTING FORCES

Fear of failing.

WHAT I MOST VALUE

1. My family — I love my sisters, they are my best friends. I love their creativity and I am so excited to work with them and learn from them. It will make our dad so proud to see us creating something together — just like when we were little girls — and making my dad proud has always been a key driving force in my life.

2. *My business – I have worked as a solopreneur for a long time. I am excited about the opportunity to build a business with my sisters – to work collaboratively towards a common goal and to have the excitement and joy of working as a team to create something special. And seriously, what's the worst thing that could happen? If it doesn't work at least I will end up with a capsule wardrobe of clothes I love, that I want to wear, that make me feel wonderful and comfortable and stylish. Winning.*

3. *My health and wellbeing – working on something so creative will enrich my life and working with my sisters will enrich my life.*

CHEER SQUAD

My sisters and my dad.

REFRAMED GOAL

It is late 2023 and my sisters and I have launched our own clothing label – Bobby Boy (named after our beautiful dad). We have delivered our first capsule wardrobe which includes a number of pieces that can be mixed and matched to create multiple outfits for women just like us – women who are struggling to find clothes that make us feel stylish, attractive, unique and which are comfortable to wear. We focus on sustainability, quality and affordability.

TAKE A STEP

1. *Register the business name.*

2. *Set up a bank account.*

3. *Start planning.*

CELEBRATE

ACKNOWLEDGE YOUR GROWTH AND LEARNINGS

EXPRESS YOUR GRATITUDE

R is for Relocate to Bali

GOAL   I want to live and work in Bali.

REFLECTION

As a 'wannabe' digital nomad, in 2017 I developed a five-year plan that would see me living and working in Bali in 2022 (at least for a few months). My thinking was this – by 2022 all of my kids would be finished high school, they would all be (young) adults and I would have less strings attaching me fulltime to Melbourne.

The plan was to base myself in Bali for three to six of Melbourne's colder months in 2022.

My plan was perfect. But then Dan got sick and along came a global pandemic.

GOAL TYPE

Go Big Goal

CHAPTER	Health & Wellbeing, Adventure, Growth, Lifestyle & Environment	DEADLINE	July 2023

RESISTING FORCES

1. Fear of being away from my kids.

2. Fear of losing clients – will my clients be happy to work with me exclusively online while I am in Bali?.

3. Lack of legal ability to stay in Bali long term.

WHAT I MOST VALUE

1. My kids — Bali is close enough for my kids to come and visit. They love Bali and they will 100 per cent be up for a free holiday.

2. My business — the silver lining afforded by the pandemic is that COVID has normalised online service delivery for my clients. For extended periods over the last few years it was literally impossible (at least in Melbourne, which had one of the most restrictive isolation protocols in the world) to work with clients face to face. And then once things opened up a little, and then a lot, engaging with clients online was suddenly the new normal. No explanations required. As a speaker during the pandemic I delivered many speaking gigs and workshops online — prior to COVID, these opportunities would have been exclusively face to face. As a coach, working online is a breeze and has opened up my business to more offshore clients. As an author, I can of course write from anywhere.

3. Excitingly the Indonesian government is launching a new 'digital nomad' visa which will allow freelancers to live in Bali, provided their earnings come from companies outside of Indonesia, for up to five years without paying taxes. In the meantime, the Indonesian government has announced that remote workers will be allowed to reside in Bali and conduct online work for up to six months.

4. My health and wellbeing — Bali is literally the health and wellbeing capital of the world.

CHEER SQUAD

My clients, my family, me!

REFRAMED GOAL

It is July 2023 and I am living and working in Bali for eight weeks. I have found a beautiful place to stay, have a local yoga and meditation studio, which has helped me meet some new friends, and I am eating fresh healthy food. I am immersing myself in the local culture, getting out on my motorbike and exploring every day. I am feeling refreshed and have been writing and creating inspiring content. I have a regular schedule of clients, and my living and working from Bali has attracted more and more like-minded women to work with me because they want to learn how to create what I have created for myself. Other businesses, entrepreneurs and digital nomads living in Bali have reached out to me to partner with them. My kids are coming to visit me. I have finally learned to surf! I love my life!

TAKE A STEP

1. *Block out July and August 2023 in my calendar.*

2. *Start putting out the feelers to contacts in Bali – declaring my intentions!.*

3. *Batch time into my calendar to research accommodation etc.*

CELEBRATE

ACKNOWLEDGE YOUR GROWTH AND LEARNINGS

EXPRESS YOUR GRATITUDE

R is for Rest and Replenish

as and when I need it and not as a gift to myself.

R is for Release

I will let go of the thoughts and the things and the possessions and the people that don't support how I want to live the rest of my life.

R is for Risks

Sometimes you just need to speculate.

R is for Reflection

and taking the time to think about what I want to do, be, give next.

R is for Renewal

Because not everything old needs to be discarded.

S is for Swim every day

GOAL — *I will swim every day for a year.*

REFLECTION

In winter it is too hard for us to dive into the sea from the rocks. The full-body immersion in one split second that is required when launching yourself off the rocks sends my brain into full-blown chaos and my mouth into a diatribe of very bad swear words.

Instead, we enter from the beach and get to experience the slow absorption method of death by one thousand cuts as the ice-cold water slowly laps over our toes to our ankles to our calves to our knees to our thighs to our fannies to our waists to our boobs, at which point we scream and plunge and swear and shriek. The fanny is the worst part. Or maybe the hands.

And then we breaststroke out to the first pole, panting little puffs of cloudy air and trying to push through the ice-cold pain as we circle the pole and breaststroke back. Some days there is a winter north wind which means we get slapped in the face by little waves the whole swim back to shore — we call these waves slappies: 'Oh no, we've got bloody slappies today...'

By the time we reach the rock wall on the return trip we are numb and exhilaration takes over. For the last two minutes of the swim we are on a high.

We run from the water with red bodies with white extremities.

We three sisters are very loud. Between the shrieking and the swearing and the laughing it is pretty clear that the Ferris girls are in the water again.

In summer things are very different. We dive into the water from the rocks and swim to the second pole. We bemoan the stingers that leave welts up our arms and legs and torsos. One day I got stung right on the fanny and continued to experience spasms of electric pain for three hours. The water is warmer and we stay in longer and it always amazes me during our summer swims how we long for winter — how we can't wait for the temperature to reach the point where the water takes our breath away and only the heartiest of swimmers go the distance. I think we are mad.

GOAL TYPE

Go Big Goal

CHAPTER	Health & Wellbeing, Adventure, Lifestyle & Environment	DEADLINE	26 December 2021 (this was one of my first ever Life List goals)

RESISTING FORCES

1. I don't like being cold or wet.

2. I don't like sand.

3. I don't like seaweed.

4. I don't want to get up early every day, especially on the weekend.

5. I really don't like being cold.

WHAT I MOST VALUE

1. My sisters: initially they were swimming without me and I wanted to be in their gang. Good old FOMO strikes again.

2. My business: like many of my goals, this will provide great fodder for content.

3. My health and wellbeing: the research is very clear on the benefits of cold-water swimming, including a euphoric swimmer's high as endorphins flood your brain; long-term improved mood and being less reactive to everyday stress; the production of good brown fat; cardio and strength building; reduced inflammation and pain, and so on. It sounds like a get well quick pill.

CHEER SQUAD

I swim with my sisters and we are a ready-made cheer squad. On any given day if one of us can't be bothered, or if two of us can't be bothered, there is always the third who says — 'Come on! Let's do this.' And so we do. There is probably no greater example to me of the power of a cheer squad than this goal, which required me to turn up day after day after day for a full year — I could not have done it without my sisters by my side.

REFRAMED GOAL

It is Christmas Day 2022 and I have swum every single day for a whole year, having started on 26 December 2021. I swam each morning with my sisters — rain, hail, or shine and without wearing a wetsuit.

TAKE A STEP

1. Set my intention.

2. Pick a date.

3. Buy new bathers.

4. Swim.

5. Swim again.

CELEBRATE

Every time I swim is a moment of joy with my sisters.

ACKNOWLEDGE YOUR GROWTH AND LEARNINGS

Over the course of the year I swam about 330 of the 365 days. In winter I wore a wetsuit top for about three weeks but then acclimated, pushed through and abandoned the top. The vast majority of the days I swam in the morning, but sometimes swam in the afternoon. In summer I often went for two to three swims a day. (And as a stretch goal – I want to swim in all five oceans around the world. So far I have swum in the Pacific, the Indian and the Atlantic oceans. That leaves the Arctic and Southern Oceans – the cold ones...)

The swimmer's high is real. There have been many mornings when at least one of the three of us girls has been feeling very overwhelmed by the shit going on in our lives on any given day, and every single day the shock of the cold water and the joy of swimming with each other completely lifts our despondency. Most mornings we scream with laughter over something one of us has done or said – most mornings we are slightly hysterical. It is exhilarating.

1. Swimming rewires my brain.

2. I still don't like being cold but I have acclimated to being cold – not just during the swims.

3. I never thought I was a morning person, but I now wake regularly at about 6.30 am and I think this is in part due to the regularity of our morning swimming routine.

4. I am a very determined woman – I now know from swimming that if I set my mind to something, I will do it – rain, hail or shine. That sort of tenacity is very empowering.

5. In winter it takes about five minutes for my body to become completely numb and for me to catch my breath. It takes about eight minutes to reach the point of enjoying the sensation of being immersed in the freezing water.

6. Swimming with my sisters every day is the greatest joy of my life — we laugh together every single day. It has brought me so much closer to them.

EXPRESS YOUR GRATITUDE

1. I am grateful for Lisa and Emma.

2. I am grateful that I live so close to the beach.

3. I am grateful for the community of other swimmers who greet me every day and are so positive and encouraging.

4. I am grateful to my dad who every morning as we depart his house (which is opposite the beach), he says 'goodbye crazy girls', and then he has hot water bottles and cups of tea ready for us at the end of the swim.

5. I am grateful for my health.

6. I am grateful when jellyfish season ends.

7. I am grateful for COVID because it gave us an extra incentive to swim every day during lockdown.

8. I am grateful for my strength of mind and determination.

9. I am grateful to have found an activity that is so good for my physical and mental health.

S is for Stop

I will stop spending money on stuff I don't need.

I will stop caring who will take the bins out.

I will stop investing my precious time on the wrong tasks.

I will stop investing my precious time on the wrong people.

I will stop sweating the small stuff.

I will stop sweating some of the big stuff.

I will stop feeling guilty for choosing takeaway over cooking.

I will stop treading water.

I will stop being complacent.

I will stop living my second best life and start living my best life.

S is for Swearing

Because I bloody love swearing.

S is for Stretch

It's all absolutely within my reach, I just need to stretch.

S is for having very good Sex

Very good.

T is for Travel as a digital nomad

GOAL	I want to travel to, live and work in countries other than Australia.

REFLECTION

This one is really important to me. I love travelling and adventure and experiencing other cultures and I see living and working overseas as the ultimate challenge for myself personally and for my business.

GOAL TYPE

Go Big Goal

CHAPTER	Health & Wellbeing, Adventure, Growth, Giving, Lifestyle & Environment	DEADLINE	July 2023 and then annually

RESISTING FORCES

1. Fear of the unknown.

2. Fear of feeling lonely.

3. Fear of losing clients.

4. Fear of being away from my kids.

WHAT I MOST VALUE

1. My business: living and working overseas will expose my business to new clients, new products and a lot of new content.

2. My health and wellbeing: I want to follow the sun. I don't like being cold and I don't want to do another Melbourne winter. Travelling and experiencing other cultures will be beautiful for my soul.

3. My growth: I want to really push myself outside my comfort zone; you only live once and I want it to be spectacular.

4. My kids: they are very welcome to come and visit me.

CHEER SQUAD

I put this one out to the world and it's amazing how many people have contacted me about it, or shared articles and updates with me about countries adopting digital nomad visas. Love it!

REFRAMED GOAL

I will embrace my inner nomad and spend three to six months of every year living and working from wherever in the world I want to live. I have accustomed my clients to working with me remotely and it is working very well — even better than I had hoped. I have picked up more clients because I am attracting like-minded digital nomads who want to learn how to design and implement their own Life Lists. I regularly write about my experiences and share my learnings to help other digital nomads and wannabe digital nomads do exactly the same. I have been picked up as an opinion columnist for at least one new content creator (maybe TV!). I am involved in the culture of the places where I live. I actively contribute to the local communities I live in and am throwing myself into making new friends. I seek out local projects to be involved in which involve community engagement, the environment, or carbon offsets. I will try anything once (except bungee jumping, which will never, ever happen. Ever). Places in my digital nomad hit list include:

- *2023: Bali — see 'R is for Relocate to Bali'*
- *2024: Italy — see 'I is for Immersion in Italy'*
- *2025: New York — because why not?*
- *2026: Let's face it — it can be anywhere I want because that is the life I am designing for myself. I can live and work absolutely anywhere in the world.*

TAKE A STEP

CELEBRATE

ACKNOWLEDGE YOUR GROWTH AND LEARNINGS

EXPRESS YOUR GRATITUDE

T is for Tattoo

Get ink baby! Stunning. Symbolic. Strong.

T is for Tenacity

There is nothing more powerful than being a cashed-up 5'ish woman with no more fucks to give.

T is for Tact

I want to be more tactful.

T is for Trailblazer

I will blaze my own trail!

T is for TED Talk

I am challenging myself to deliver a TED Talk.

U is for Unlock
new experiences

GOAL   *Experiences over possessions.*

REFLECTION

I am over gifting my kids 'stuff' for Christmas and birthdays. They have enough stuff. And gifting them more stuff just adds to all the stuff that sits around the house and on the floor and on the coach and on the dining table and in my way.

I am going to gift experiences over possessions and tapping into my kids' innate competitiveness seems a good place to start.

My kids are ridiculously competitive. From the time Wally could crawl he was trying to keep up with Freddie. Then when Peggy came along she literally taught herself to walk at 10 months of age so that she wouldn't miss out on anything. When they were little they would compete over who could run fastest, climb highest, kick the longest, carry the most, hold their breath the longest, eat the quickest, jump the highest, break the most bones (Wally won that one), have the most stitches (on one unforgettable day Freddie and Peggy each had separate hospital visits for stitches arising from completely different accidents).

These days it's more about who is the smartest, works the most, works the least, earns the most, earns the least, is the strongest, can drink the most, can stay up the latest, can party the hardest, is the tallest. It is never ending.

But what this super competitiveness does is that it creates a great platform for my gifting experiences (rather than possessions) where my kids can compete to their very last breath.

I will also throw in some noncompetitive stuff too.

GOAL TYPE

Go Small Goal

| CHAPTER | *Lifestyle & Environment, Giving* | DEADLINE | *Immediate* |

RESISTING FORCES

My kids might push for possessions. Too bad.

WHAT I MOST VALUE

1. My kids and time spent with them having fun and creating memories.

2. Not accumulating more crap.

CHEER SQUAD

My kids!

REFRAMED GOAL

In line with my decluttering passion (see 'D is for Declutter') and my emission reduction goal (see 'Z is for Zero out my carbon footprint'), I will gift the people I love experiences and not possessions.

TAKE A STEP

1. Research cool experiences.

2.

3.

4.

5.

CELEBRATE

The experiences themselves are a celebration!

ACKNOWLEDGE YOUR GROWTH AND LEARNINGS

1. Christmas two years ago I gifted the kids, the boys' girlfriends, myself and my dad gift cards for go-kart racing. The competition was fierce. I am pretty sure I came last — in fact I know I did — and my dad pulled out even before it began because to be fair it did look pretty hairy. My kids were brutal and merciless, and the boys' girlfriends were no less so. We bloody loved it. It was wonderful spending time together doing something that was just so much fun. We all left on a high and have created a wonderful memory.

2. Last Christmas I gifted everyone a paintball experience. Hilarious. For the full story on what transpired you can read my Life List blog at www.katechristie.com.au.

3. For Wally's twenty-first birthday I took him to see Andrea Bocelli. Wally has always loved opera — when he was 10 and singing opera in the shower he fainted after holding a note for too long. God knows what he was thinking but I'm pretty sure his fainting was as a result of a competition with his brother over who could hold a note the longest. We got very dressed up (think 'Pretty Woman at the Opera'). I loved having that experience with Wally. Another memory I will treasure.

4. For Peggy's nineteenth birthday I took her to Byron Bay to get her hippie on. We swam, watched the sunset, chose a beautiful restaurant for her birthday dinner and she got the best bedroom. Perfect.

5. I want to look back on my life, each and every year, and remember experiences not possessions. Accumulating experiences is so much more fulfilling than accumulating stuff.

EXPRESS YOUR GRATITUDE

1. I am grateful for my kids and my family.

2. I am grateful that my kids want to hang out with me and do fun stuff.

3. I am grateful that I have created a life where I have invested the time to learn how to be time affluent so that I can engage in these experiences.

4. I am grateful that I have the perspective that allows me to prioritise these experiences with my family.

5. I am grateful that I have my health.

6. I am grateful for my wonderful life.

U is for Unplug

Hiking more has taught me first hand the simple pleasure of unplugging and making myself completely unavailable. I will do more of this. Even when I am not hiking and out of range – I will actively and regularly put myself out of range.

U is for being Unafraid

and unstoppable, unique, unlimited, undeniable, unbeatable, unwavering – I am so bloody excited about the rest of my life!

Vis for Valuing what I most value

GOAL	*I will prioritise what I most value in my life.*

REFLECTION

Over the last few years I have come to realise that there is a big difference between my Values (the behaviours I live by) and what I most value (the people and experiences I want to invest most of my time in). It's important for me to place value on both my Values and on what I most value.

GOAL TYPE

Go Small Goal

CHAPTER	*Health & Wellbeing, Wealth, Adventure, Growth, Giving, Relationships, Lifestyle & Environment*	DEADLINE	*Ongoing*

RESISTING FORCES

None.

WHAT I MOST VALUE

1. The three things I most value are: my family; my business; my health and wellbeing.

2. Spending the vast majority of my time with the people I most value and on the experiences I most value.

CHEER SQUAD

Just me.

REFRAMED GOAL

I will design and build my life around what I most value. I will:

- *Love my kids every single minute*
- *See my dad every day*
- *Spend time with my sisters*
- *Listen to myself*
- *Not waste my time because my time is precious*
- *Work with focus and play with abandon*
- *Honour my posse of incredible women*
- *Celebrate myself*
- *Respect my own boundaries*
- *Give, but not to the point where I have nothing left to give myself*
- *Accept that I can't control how you act but I can control how I react*
- *Tell my kids that I love them every single day even when they are shitting me*
- *Cuddle and kiss my kids every chance I get*
- *Know my value — I am a prize and I do not need to prove my worth to anyone*
- *Stop compromising*
- *Sleep a lot*
- *Help other people design and live their best lives*
- *Always say I love you to the people I love*
- *Never go to bed angry*
- *Just be me.*

TAKE A STEP

1. Actively batch my calendar with the people and experiences I most value.

2. Say NO to the people and experiences that do not align with what I most value.

3.

4.

5.

CELEBRATE

By mastering every moment to live an audacious life.

ACKNOWLEDGE YOUR GROWTH AND LEARNINGS

1. *I do have the strength, wisdom and discipline to prioritise what I most value.*

2. *Discipline is key – I need to keep reminding myself to stay the course.*

3. *It's okay to say no.*

EXPRESS YOUR GRATITUDE

1. *I am grateful that I have the strength, wisdom and discipline to prioritise what I most value.*

2. *I am grateful that I have invested the time to get this right for me.*

V is for Versatile

My Life List isn't locked in stone. It will change and evolve and grow and shrink depending on me and what is happening around me. But it will always be a constant in my life. I will never stop designing my perfect life.

V is for Vulnerable

and being more so and not being afraid to let people in.

W is for Woo Woo

GOAL	*I will embrace a little more woo woo.*
REFLECTION	

I was eight years old when my mum informed us that she was a witch.

We were living in England, the perfect place for a modern-day witch to indulge in a little historical witch hunting. One day as we toured a house of some historical significance or other my mum recoiled on entering the butler's pantry attached to a kitchen. She could hear crying, she stated. 'Can you hear the crying?', she asked. 'Can you feel how cold it is in here?'

At this point I'm pretty sure everyone on the tour was suddenly feeling cold because my mum had creeped us the fuck out.

The guide looked at my mum with respect (as the rest of us backed away) and shared that there had been a number of sightings associated with the room over the centuries. Hundreds of years ago, the guide stated, it was said that a little girl had been locked in a cupboard as punishment and that she had been forgotten and had died. It had repeatedly been reported that the house was haunted and that people could hear a small child crying.

Pretty. Scary. Shit. Thanks Mum.

We spent weekends retracing the sites and stories of the witch hunts of the sixteenth and seventeenth centuries. Mum declared that as a witch herself there was no doubt that if she had lived 500 years ago she would have been thrown into a pond with her right thumb tied to her left big toe to testify as to her witchy status. If she floated she would indeed be judged a witch and would burn at the stake. If she sank and drowned she would be declared innocent — albeit dead.

Another telltale sign of being a witch, she shared, was if you had the 'Devil's Mark' — anything from a large mole to a flea bite — on your body.

It just so happened that I had, and continue to this day to have, a rather large mole not so far from my fanny. As a child it was awkward and embarrassing and simply horrifying to have a mole on your fannywandango. My parents had always kindly reassured me this mole was in fact a beauty spot — and I was very, very lucky to have a beautiful vagina. I bought into that one — I mean, come on, I was a kid.

My older sister, however, was delighted. She seized on to the whole Devil's Mark thing and quite relentlessly assured me I too was a witch because only a witch would have a mole on her witchy vagina. It was hard to argue with her logic.

I had nightmares for months.

Eventually my mum stopped talking so often about being a witch — I think she was sick of my sleepless nights. But she didn't stop doing her witchy shit on the quiet — years later, after she passed away, we found the names of all of the people she felt had wronged her and her family scripted on small pieces of parchment and frozen in ice-cube trays in the freezer. I'm pretty sure she also made voodoo dolls, but let's not go there.

I do not believe in God and up until quite recently, I have never been particularly spiritual.

The big spiritual shift occurred for me after my marriage broke down. I was frightened and angry. I was terrified that I would have to give up my small business and go back to the workforce to support myself. I loved my small business, but the fact was that it was super small and not anywhere near making me enough money to qualify as a liveable income. My ex-husband called it a hobby and suggested it might be time for me to get a real job again.

I remember the day very clearly. I was driving my car towards my house. I had the windows all the way down. It was very cold but I felt like I needed the wind and the chill to in some way whip through the car, whip through my brain, and blow away the crap that was circling in my head.

Universe, I yelled at the top of my lungs out the window, I know I have never believed in you, but please help me. I don't want to get a job. I want my business to work. I want to help as many people as possible. But I need your help right now. Please help me. Please, please — just throw me a bone.

And the universe did.

Two days later I received an email from a new client about a new project. A big client. A big project. I had been thrown a bone and I grabbed it and ran. I threw myself and my sadness and my grief into my business. And my business exploded.

I honestly live by my pledge to help as many people as possible. First because I love what I do, but second because I made a deal with the Universe and the Universe delivered and I promised to hold up my end of the bargain too.

GOAL TYPE

Go Big Goal

CHAPTER	Health & Wellbeing, Adventure, Growth, Lifestyle & Environment	DEADLINE	Now

RESISTING FORCES

Fear of the unknown, primarily. I have always wanted to see a clairvoyant for example — but what if she sees something awful, or something pretty ho-hum; or what if she doesn't see anything at all?

WHAT I MOST VALUE

Being curious, learning, increasing my knowledge, being open to growth.

CHEER SQUAD

Whoever is crazy enough to come along for the ride.

My mum would have backed me on this one big time.

REFRAMED GOAL

I am curious about the universe as energy and I will actively explore this in multiple ways. I will read about it, set new intentions, and seek out new experience such as seeing a clairvoyant, trying sound healing, and looking at more holistic concepts of health and wellness. I won't be closed off to what I might think of as unusual without first giving it a go.

TAKE A STEP

1. Think about what I want to explore.

2. Research opportunities.

3. Jump.

4.

5.

CELEBRATE

It's fun. Just enjoy it. Celebrate it by doing more of it.

ACKNOWLEDGE YOUR GROWTH AND LEARNINGS

1. The Sound Healer:

I'll admit it, I was dubious.

In the past I have failed miserably at meditation. I have never, ever been able to quiet my busy mind. I breathe deeply for two minutes and my brain goes to a place of lists, to dos, past wrongs, current issues, future plans — nothing about meditation has ever worked for me. If anything I find it frustrating and time wasting and it is impossible to sit still and just be. I am very impatient.

But there I was, after my normal bed time, in a yoga studio, under a particularly noisy pool hall, down a dodgy-looking lane in Fitzroy, lying on a mat in the dark, covered by a blanket as our healer explained the journey we were about to take. Our bodies, he explained, have vibrational frequencies that are affected and can be balanced by sound. Set your intentions for the session, he requested, and relax and enjoy. Some of you will feel deep healing, others will simply relax. Go with the flow of your own personal experience.

I set my intentions which included being open to the experience and — best case scenario — tapping into some greater power that would tell me all of the answers to all of my questions and solve all of my issues and deliver me ongoing inner happiness. Forever.

It was a big ask — but I am at the point where it I'm all about Going Big or Going Back to Bed.

From the second I closed my eyes and the healer struck the first Tibetan bowl I felt my body and, more importantly, my mind relax. He sang and chanted with a beautiful, deep resonance that literally made my body tingle. He rang gongs that caused my body to flex and then relax as I felt the tension drain away. At one stage he placed a vibrating bowl onto my stomach and it took me somewhere else completely in my brain. I had visions. I'm not kidding. I saw myself on a beach dancing with a man who I could not see in detail, but when he wrapped his arms around me I felt such a deep sense of calm and safety.

Loved it. Will be doing it again.

2. The Clairvoyant:

I met her at a Wellness Fair. There were a number of clairvoyants to choose from and I liked her face the most. I paid my $70 for my 20-minute ride and asked if I could tape the reading so that I wouldn't miss a thing. I have listened to that recording many times.

I set my intentions and away we went.

Regardless of whether you believe in this stuff, my session with the clairvoyant was very, very good for my soul. It was uplifting and delightful and heartening and gave me so much optimism for my future that I walked away feeling empowered and focused.

I don't know whether what she saw or read in the cards will play out in the way that she said that it would, but maybe that's not important—she told a compelling story, each card seemed to build on the next and I was left with such a wonderfully positive and powerful frame of mind that I may well just make it all happen through sheer force of will.

And maybe that's all that it takes.

3. Woo Woo is fun. I'll be doing more of it.

EXPRESS YOUR GRATITUDE

1. I am grateful that I have an open and curious mind.

2. I am grateful for the incredibly learned minds that share their thoughts on energy and the universe and spirituality as I am learning a lot from you.

3. I am grateful that my mum was a witch.

W is for being Well Travelled

My top Life List destinations on my to do in the next few years are:

- Peru
- Morocco
- Mexico
- Bali
- Italy
- Turkey
- Croatia
- Africa

- Denmark
- Nepal
- India
- America
- The Arctic
- Greenland
- More of Australia

W is for Wild

We all need to be a little untamed from time to time.

X is for X-ing out alcohol

GOAL	*I will stop drinking alcohol.*
REFLECTION	

After Dan left I fell into the habit of rewarding myself with a glass of wine most nights. And that fairly quickly turned into the habit of having a glass of wine every night. And then a few glasses. And, quite comfortably and without any effort at all, I fell into the habit of having half a bottle of wine a night.

It wasn't social drinking. It was anti-social drinking. It was 'all on my own, indulge yourself, you deserve it' kind of drinking.

At some point I realised that what had started as a little reward for getting to the end of the day had become a need — a process of watching the clock click towards 5 pm so I could have a drink. And I didn't like that feeling or that dependency.

I didn't like what it did to my sleep, or my skin or my self-worth. It actually made me feel like shit — every morning I would wake full of self-recrimination and I would vow that I would not have a drink that night ... but by around 3 pm I would have fully turned my thinking around and into some sort of self-justification that I deserved to have a drink after all. Just one.

My self-talk the next morning was awful.

And so after about 18 months of this I went cold turkey and I stopped drinking for six months. It was really hard to break the habit. But the benefits were tangible — I slept like a dream, I woke without guilt and I felt so much better about myself.

So much better, in fact, that I decided it would be okay to indulge myself in a glass or two of wine again — but just on the weekends. And that worked to the extent that it was just a glass or two on the weekends, but my sleep went to shit, my stomach played up, my anxiety surged, I had more nightmares, and I woke feeling guilty — all over again.

GOAL TYPE

Go Small Goal

CHAPTER	*Health & Wellbeing, Growth, Lifestyle & Environment*	DEADLINE	*September*

RESISTING FORCES

Literally none, except that little voice I sometimes, but thankfully not always, get at 5 pm nudging me to maybe just have one glass of wine.

WHAT I MOST VALUE

1. Feeling in control of my willpower.

2. Feeling good about myself.

3. My physical health and mental wellbeing.

4. My sleep.

5. My self-worth.

CHEER SQUAD

My sisters.

REFRAMED GOAL

I am not going to drink alcohol any more.

TAKE A STEP

1. Set my intention.

2. Reschedule my calendar to ensure I am exercising at 'wine-o-clock.'

3. Create a new nightly ritual - a hot bath and book.

4. Find a tea I love to brew.

5. Stay consistent.

6. Make the decision once.

CELEBRATE

Every morning when I wake feeling great!

ACKNOWLEDGE YOUR GROWTH AND LEARNINGS

1. I don't enjoy drinking any more. It doesn't make me feel great or even good. It makes me feel the exact opposite of this.

2. I don't really like the taste of alcohol.

3. I don't like how drinking makes me feel, particularly the self-recrimination.

4. I love undisturbed sleep.

5. I love not having the guilt each morning after succumbing to a few glasses of wine the night before.

EXPRESS YOUR GRATITUDE

1. I am grateful to have removed alcohol as a choice from my day: not drinking alcohol at all is a much easier decision than sometimes drinking alcohol because I only had to make the 'I'm not drinking' decision once as opposed to each night.

2. I am grateful to have great sleep again.

3. I am grateful that I have removed the source of a lot of negative self-talk.

4. I am grateful that I have my health and I am focusing on being the best version of me.

5. I am grateful that I get out of bed feeling rested and without recrimination.

X is for kisses

Kiss passionately. There is seriously nothing better than a steaming hot kiss.

X is for Xoompin

I'm all for going full throttle over any bumps in the road.

Y is for the Yes Quest

GOAL	Say Yes for a whole month.
REFLECTION	

It was my second date with a man who I ended up going on exactly three dates with. We had agreed to go for a walk — which for most people would be pretty simple — let's just meet and go for a walk. But not me. This required some planning.

A week before the date I sent a text to my date that read something along the lines of:

We could walk from Brighton Beach to St Kilda Beach — it's about 7 km. We could meet at one end and park one car and then drive the other car to the other end and park that car and then walk back to the start and collect the first car and then drive back to pick up the second car.

WTAF? Is it any wonder we only went on three dates? Poor bloke.

I am a planner. I organise. It makes sense that I am a time management and productivity specialist, but seriously, sometimes I really just need to go with the flow and chill the fuck out.

And so, I add to my Life List the need for a little spontaneity. Not everything needs to be planned to within an inch of its life.

Knowing that this one was going to be very, very hard for me and well outside my comfort zone, it was important for me to share the goal with friends — my cheer squad — so that they could keep me accountable. There is a very good reason why I included appointing a cheer squad as a step in The Master Every Moment Framework — when you share your goal with your cheer squad, you make yourself accountable and you turn what would otherwise be an internal deadline into an external deadline. This strategy massively increases your chances of turning up and getting shit done.

Having set a particular month as the month where I was going to start saying Yes spontaneously for a whole month (the irony of scheduling when I was going to start acting all spontaneous is not lost on me, but knowing myself I still needed to have an element of control over the uncontrollable), I shared my new mindset with one of my best friends.

This wonderful woman is a life force. She is a whirlwind. Her mantra is that she will try anything — ANYTHING — for an hour. Who better to keep me accountable to my goal? Who better to be my chief cheerleader?

I had only one rule for the Yes Quest: If someone invites me to do something I have to say Yes. No excuses.

GOAL TYPE

Go Now Goal

CHAPTER	DEADLINE
Adventure, Growth	August

RESISTING FORCES

1. Fear of not being in control.

2. Fear of putting myself too far out of my comfort zone.

3. Lack of energy.

WHAT I MOST VALUE

1. Mixing things up a little.

2. Actually pushing myself outside of my comfort zone (it's one of my Go Big Goal rules, I mean, come on Kate!).

3. Actually experiencing things that are new — I can't always set my own agenda with this, I need to be genuinely open to opportunities that I wouldn't normally consider.

4. Living my best life.

CHEER SQUAD

Sharing this goal proved critical — I needed to tell the people who I knew would then invite me to do lots and lots of things I would otherwise never, ever, not in a million years consider doing.

REFRAMED GOAL

It is August and I have set the intention of saying Yes to every single opportunity that comes my way for the entire month. I am not allowed to say no.

TAKE A STEP

1. Set my intention.

2. Declare my goal to my naughty mates and kids.

3. Say Yes.

4.

5.

CELEBRATE

I celebrated the fact that I did it, I mostly loved it and I learned a lot from it. I celebrated at the waterpark big time. I celebrated kicking over to September and being able to say no again, but maybe less than I used to.

ACKNOWLEDGE YOUR GROWTH AND LEARNINGS

1. Just say yes. I will be doing more of it and I will also have more Yes Quest months where I have to say yes for the whole month, regardless.

2. Life is very, very awesome when you engage in random acts of spontaneity.

3. If you can't afford travel insurance, you can't afford to travel.

4. While all of the activities I took part in doing my first Yes Quest met three of my four goal rules (each was challenging; outside my comfort zone; and new) and I would not have contemplated doing most of them but for the Yes Quest, each and every one of them turned out to be absolutely glorious — hence unwittingly and surprisingly also meeting my fourth goal rule.

5. My sense of enthusiasm for the Yes Quest became contagious and self-fulfilling and I am now much more readily saying yes to things I used to say no to. This is a big shift for me.

A sample of my experiences:

1. The 30 m drop

One in all in.

We were in Bali at the start of my Yes Quest, which in retrospect was not entirely sensible timing on my part. The kids (all young adults but still very much kids at heart) wanted to spend the day at a waterpark. I was on for it and promised that I would go on every single ride with them. I was, after all, on a Yes Quest.

My kids are thrillseekers. I know this. And generally speaking I am too, particularly when it comes to rollercoasters and rides where you are strapped in with a metal pole and a big fat seat belt. But at a waterpark, there are no seat belts.

There is no starting small with my kids and then building up. Our first ride was 30 m high. After climbing to the heavens, and passing a sign that read 'Slide at Your Own Risk' and another that was tucked slightly out of sight and which politely read 'One moment please — rescue in progress', I was surprised to see no queue at all at the top of the slide. Later I realised that this was because we were literally the only lunatics in the whole place who were prepared to give the ride a go.

The perspex glass opened and after handing over my glasses for safekeeping I stepped into what can only be described as a vertical coffin on top of tube that dropped 30 metres to the earth. The coffin door closed and I was literally freaking the fuck out.

The kids were chanting my name. The water was spilling down my back. The ride attendant was smiling like a maniac. A creepy as hell digital voice sounded within the coffin: '5, 4, 3, 2, 1' and then the fucking floor dropped away. Gone.

I plunged like a boulder, screaming my lungs out and I don't think I stopped screaming until we exited the waterpark four hours later.

The kids thought I was a legend. I lost a good five years from my life.

Whose idea was the Yes Quest for god's sake?

2. Speed Date Night:

Knowing my new philosophy and that I was in the midst of a Yes Quest, my cheeky bestie asked me to go speed dating with her. I wanted to vomit. This one was way, way too far outside my comfort zone.

It was a Yes from me.

With increasing anxiety I sent her multiple vomiting emojis as the date night approached, but I knew that both she and I would not let me back out. Rules are rules. For more on my speed dating experience, see Part 2: MOMENTum.

Will I ever do it again? Not on your life.

3. A random Yes to a man in the jungle

We were in Bali and Peggy was keen to explore some of the famous waterfalls dotted around Ubud. After a little research we chose two quite well-known spectacular waterfalls, Kanto Lampo and Tibumana, and then after checking Google Earth and working out whether it would be a lunatic idea to try and get there ourselves on a motorbike (yes, it would be) or whether it would be worth paying a driver to take us there (another yes), we threw in a third, apparently lesser known waterfall and set off to be thrilled.

Kanto Lampo was wonderful—an Instagram influencer's dream and, so it would seem, the dream of every other tourist in Bali who has a mobile phone and an Instagram account. Luckily we arrived early and got to enjoy standing under the steady flow of the waterfall pretty much on our own for a few minutes. Within 10 minutes, however, we were joined by a steady and consistent stream of loved-up couples. We spent a highly enjoyable half hour watching each couple re-create the exact same photo kissing under the waterfall with the girl's leg jauntily cocked in the air at the knee. Peggy was asked to be photographer by many couples and seriously, she should have charged for her time.

Next stop, the lesser known falls. When we arrived I was thrilled to see no loved-up couples in the empty field (a.k.a. car park), and the lack of an entrance fee seemed to indicate that this place is, at least for now, not yet an influencer's paradise.

We descended the many steps to the river and followed the signs to the waterfall. We were completely alone as we arrived at our destination, but for a Balinese man who, rising from the waters, greeted us and explained that as one of the local custodians of the river it was his job to help us physically navigate our way across the rocks without dying—terrific.

He instructed us to remove our shoes, grab hold of the rope attached to the rocks beside the apparently death-inspiring cascade, and hoist ourselves up the rocks and along the top of the waterfall. So far so good.

The waterfall, he explained, emanated from a very spiritual and hidden part of the river upstream. If we had time, he said, as a local community member he could take us up the river to this spiritual place that most tourists never get to see. It would take only 30 minutes.

I'm not going to lie — I know when I am being sold a line, so we politely declined. Plus I've seen enough horror movies to know for damn sure that you never, ever follow the strange man off the beaten track into the jungle when no-one on earth knows where you are or what time you are due back. But then I remembered I was on the Yes Quest and, personal safety aside and disregarding the personal safety of my daughter, wasn't this exactly the sort of opportunity I was supposed to be saying Yes to?

But, without pressing us further, our friendly river custodian guided us to scoot along our bums into the middle of the waterfall. As we slipped and slid over algae-covered rocks through the cascade of water and desperately clung to our bikinis, he merrily and unnecessarily called, 'Mind your pants!'. Once we were positioned mid stream, he asked for my phone and proceeded to take a dozen photos and create the most incredible slow motion reel of us screaming in delight as the waterfall pummelled through and over us. It was simply joyful. I have never laughed so much in my life.

Trust built, fun had, we agreed to head off into the jungle with our new friend in search of the spiritual place not available to tourists. I am, after all, all about saying Yes right now.

What proceeded will absolutely feature in the movie of my life where I am played by Laura Dern or Reese Witherspoon or perhaps Julia Roberts.

As we tramped along the jungle path with nothing but the calls of birds, the whisper of a quiet breeze and the movement of vines and green, green, green everywhere, our guide produced a portable speaker from his backpack and the peace of the jungle was interrupted by loud, tinny techno music which I have to say dampened the vibe slightly. Sensing we weren't a techno crowd, our guide swiftly lowered the volume, declared that what we really needed for our spiritual walk was an 'internationally famous' song and he switched the dial to a musical arrangement of 'My Heart Will Go On'.

Peggy and I exchanged delighted looks.

We descended the path to the river and were instructed to keep our thongs on, grab a long bamboo pole and enter the river. Follow my footsteps exactly, our guide instructed, it can be slippery and there are sinkholes and people unfamiliar with the river have fallen and died and there are poisonous plants and people unfamiliar with the river have stepped on them and died and it is not good for the spirituality of the river when people die. No shit.

As Celine assured us that our hearts would in fact go on, we wandered up the brown river dwarfed on either side by thick impenetrable jungle. It was incredible. To begin with the water was shin deep, but as we progressed up the river we waded knee and then thigh deep with our sarongs trailing in the water as we navigated our way around the sinkholes and kept our balance across slippery rocks with the use of our poles.

We were completely alone but for our guide and the 2-m-long snake Peggy saw exiting the water and slithering up the opposite bank. Unperturbed, our guide produced a home whittled flute from his backpack and proceeded to accompany Celine. I promise you that I am not making any of this up.

We walked for a good 20 minutes, with water now waist deep, before turning a bend to see the jungle replaced by two sheer cliff walls down which a stunning drop waterfall plunged. The guide asked for my phone again and snapped photos as Peggy and I walked through the waterfall, and waded around another bend surrounded by walls of rock and plunging vines to find a second waterfall under which the locals had rigged up a swing from the vines.

Of course we went on the swing.

The experience was magnificent, surreal. Our guide explained that he was very good with mobile phone pictures and videos and I later found he had created slow motion videos of us on the swing, which I am so going to edit to be accompanied by Celine Dion. I absolutely promise that by the time you read this, you can go to my Life List blog on my website (www.katechristie.com.au) and the video will be there. I hope you enjoy it as much as we did.

This is exactly what the Yes Quest was supposed to be all about.

As we parted, our guide pressed us not to share the location of the spiritual river. He wants it to stay hidden, not commercialised, not ruined by big tourism, and only available to the lucky few who stumble across it by chance and are brave enough to say yes to a bloke in a sarong playing a flute.

EXPRESS YOUR GRATITUDE

1. I am very grateful that I took on the Yes Quest because it exposed me to very new things and I learned a lot about myself.

2. I am grateful for the new experiences that were genuinely fun.

3. I am grateful that I have built the sort of relationship with my kids where they want to spend time with me.

4. I am grateful that my kids think I am awesome.

5. I am grateful that I never, ever have to go speed dating again — which puts speed dating right up there with skiing.

Z is for Zero out my carbon footprint

GOAL	To be much more conscious about my impact on the environment.

REFLECTION

I am far too complacent. Walking the Larapinta Trail and watching and participating in the very mindful practice of recycling and carrying all of our waste out of the pristine desert was very impactful for me. I can and should be doing a lot more.

GOAL TYPE

Go Small Goal for now but this may turn into a Go Big Goal (it's burning away in the back of my brain).

CHAPTER	Lifestyle & Environment, Growth	DEADLINE	Immediate

RESISTING FORCES

1. Lack of focus and prioritisation.

2. Lack of time to research the options.

WHAT I MOST VALUE

1. Ensuring my kids and their kids and theirs can live a long, safe, clean, healthy life.

2. Minimising my impact on others.

CHEER SQUAD

Just me for this one.

REFRAMED GOAL

I am more climate conscious.

At a practical level, I take steps each day to reduce my personal climate impact by walking to and from the shops instead of driving; actively recycling instead of being lazy and throwing all my waste into one bin; acquiring less and where possible acquiring secondhand; avoiding fast fashion; eating less meat; buying local; and reducing my energy consumption.

Recognising that many of my Life List goals involve travelling to other countries and travelling within other countries, for each trip I take I will support local or global projects that help cut carbon, remove carbon or contribute to benefits for vulnerable communities.

I will research and donate to evidence-based projects run by high impact organisations that operate with transparency and the highest levels of environmental integrity.

I will take out annual subscriptions with organisations that are third party verified.

TAKE A STEP

CELEBRATE

ACKNOWLEDGE YOUR GROWTH AND LEARNINGS

EXPRESS YOUR GRATITUDE

Z is for catching as many zzzzzzzzz's as possible

I love sleeping. I will continue to prioritise sleep and get an average of nine hours sleep a night.

Z is for my Zest for life!

I live a life where I master every moment and live an audacious life. Because life is too short not to.

Thank you

Thank you for reading *The Life List: Master Every Moment and Live an Audacious Life*.

I hope that it has given you the spark you need to embrace Moments and to generate Momentum and to create a life by design that is absolutely Momentous.

I hope that it has given you the courage to embrace the exquisite joy of becoming unapologetically selfish. Or at least a little less selfless.

Thank you to the wonderful women who generously invested your precious time to share with me how you feel about this next stage of your lives. You are amazing.

Thank you to Lucy Raymond, Chris Shorten, Renee Aurish, Allison Hiew, Clare Dowdell and the whole team at Wiley for continuing to work with me and helping to spread my words. I am so grateful for your support and guidance.

Thank you to my dad, Bob, and my sisters, Lisa and Emma, for your unflinching support and love and laughter. We are a tight little unit.

Thank you most of all to my incredibly brave, smart, resilient and funny kids — Freddie, Wally and Peggy — for keeping me on my toes, making me laugh, annoying the hell out of me, distracting me and encouraging me. Thank you for keeping me young and ageing me all at once. Thank you for choosing me to be your mum. I love you more and more and more. The end.

Kate x

About Kate

Kate Christie is a time management expert, global speaker, coach and bestselling author. She is a single mum to three amazing kids who fill her heart with a lot of joy and moments of ridiculously intense stress.

In 2020 Kate's ex-husband and the dad to her kids was diagnosed with pancreatic cancer. Dan died in April 2021. Losing Dan was a catalyst for Kate to live her best life. To fast forward all of the huge, audacious living she had planned to get to at some stage—to right now. In September 2021 Kate shared the first iteration of her 'Life List' with *CEOWORLD Magazine*—a list of things Kate was going to do, as soon as possible, while she was still young enough to enjoy them. Because life is too short not to live your best life.

Kate's Life List prompted a huge response from people around the world wanting to live their best life right now and it helped form the inspiration for this book.

Kate has a reputation for helping her clients find 30-plus hours of lost time. After dedicating the last 10 years of her business life to productivity and time management, Kate wants to help her readers take the next step in their relationship with time—now that you have your time back and under control, what exactly are you going to do with it?

Some of the things that Kate is most proud of:

- Her kids who are simply awesome and wonderful and kind and fun and who still haven't moved out of the house despite lots of encouragement

- Her relationship with her sisters and her dad who she sees every day unless she is travelling

- Helping thousands of people around the world to regain control of their time

- Working with incredible women to inspire them to set their intention to live a life by design and to create and implement their own Life List

- Having written and published five books and being a best selling author

- Being both a self-published author (books one to three) and a published author with Wiley (books four and five)

- Speaking to audiences around the world from Australia to America to the UK to Western Europe to Asia to Eastern Europe

- Living her own audacious life by design.

Because life is too short not to.

Please connect with Kate and let her know how your Life List is going:

Mail: kc@katechristie.com.au
Web: www.katechristie.com.au
LinkedIn: www.linkedin.com/in/kate-christie/
Facebook: www.facebook.com/kate.christie.92
Instagram: @KateChristieloves

Do you want to work with me?

Having worked for years as a lawyer—both in legal firms and in-house in Australia's largest telecommunications company—as a senior executive in operational roles, and run my own businesses, all while managing a family and for the last six years being a single mum, I have a very broad and very deep skill set across many aspects of big and small business and across work and life.

I've coached thousands of individuals and teams on time management, productivity, goal setting, life by design, business (big and small) planning, speaking with confidence, impression management, brand management and more. I have spoken in front of audiences in Australia, Asia, America, Western Europe, the UK and Eastern Europe. I have written five books and I am a bestselling author.

You can work with me via 1:1 coaching, group coaching, workshops, speaking engagements and retreats to develop or sharpen your skills, solve problems, reach facilitated outcomes, take advantage of specific opportunities or design your dream work and personal life.

If you are feeling inspired to start getting your time under control or if you are ready to design and implement your own Life List, there are a number of ways we can work together. Read through the information on the following pages or reach out to me direct at kc@katechristie.com.au. You can also connect with me on Facebook, LinkedIn and Instagram.

The Life List Program

If you loved this book and you are feeling inspired to write and implement your own Life List, sign up for my Life List Program which is designed to help women make the transition from the life you are living right now to your magnificent life by design.

Option 1: You will be part of a group of like-minded women who will work directly with me where I will inspire and motivate you with my unique, down-to-earth and very candid style.

Option 2: You can have me all to yourself with 1:1 coaching.

You can read more about The Life List Program at www.katechristie .com.au or email me at kc@katechristie.com.au if you are ready to discuss the program in more detail.

The Life List Retreat

Looking for a dramatic injection of inspiration? My Life List Retreats are designed to get you away from your day-to-day environment so that you can truly and exclusively focus on yourself. If you need the headspace away from your family or your work or your shopping list or your to-do list or you simply want to luxuriate in being 'yourself' for a few days, then join me for some massive self-indulgence.

This is a no-apology 'Me First' experience that is 100 per cent all about you.

Each Life List Retreat has limited availability to ensure that you get as much of me and the other inspiring women as possible. You will have all the time in the world. Time just for you. Time to:

- reflect on your life to date and everything you have achieved

- set your intentions for the next chapter of your life

- craft your own magnificent Life List

- prioritise at least one Go Big Goal

- map out your Go Big Goal, ready for implementation

- work with me and the rest of the group

- work with me 1:1

- choose to participate in activities such as exercise, massage or meditation

- spend time with other like-minded incredibly inspiring women

- spend time on your own to reflect, refresh and reframe

- immerse yourself in your awesomeness.

You can read more about the Life List Retreat at www.katechristie .com.au or email me at kc@katechristie.com.au for an application form.

Time management and executive/ business coaching

If it's time to reshape your career, or grow your business, or take time out to be with your family, or to shift direction, or to simply maximise your productivity, the first thing you need to do is to make sure you control your time. When you have control of your time, you have control of the agenda.

I will work with you 1:1 to step you through my proven 5 SMART Step Framework to ensure you have all the strategies you need to put yourself back in the driver's seat in your life.

I am an extremely passionate and focused coach and I will give you 100 per cent of my time and expertise so that you achieve your goals and objectives, and to ensure you understand the time management and productivity strategies you need to implement.

For more information about this program check out my website at www .katechristie.com.au or email me at kc@katechristie.com.au to arrange a call to make sure we have the right chemistry to smash this out of the park.

Speaker for your next event

'Kate is a storyteller—she told our audience at the start that she wanted to leave them educated, entertained and with a lasting impact on the way they choose to live, work and play, and she delivered. The attendee feedback from the event consistently rated Kate as one of the stand out presenters from the conference.'

Luke Renehan, Head of Marketing and Events, Newable, United Kingdom

Engage me to speak live or virtually at your next event or retreat. You can read more about my current Speaking and Workshop Topics, download my Speakers Kit, watch reels from previous events and explore the many amazing testimonials from previous events on my website at www .katechristie.com.au.

If you would like to discuss your next event please email me at kc@katechristie.com.au.

Do you want to partner with me?

I regularly partner with amazing brands and businesses on win-win outcomes that add value to my clients and readers and which add value to your customers. If you are interested in discussing partnership opportunities that allow you to expose your brand to my clients and readers—think experiences, adventures, travel and lifestyle opportunities that women will want to add to their Life Lists, or think of how I can add value to your clients with my knowledge and experience, then please email me at kc@katechristie.com.au.

Buy this book in bulk

Who doesn't want to design their perfect life? For the perfect gift for your business customers or your own team or for audience members at your next event, contact me at kc@katechristie.com.au to order this book in bulk at special bulk discount prices.

There are a few ways I can package up bulk orders for you, including personally signing every copy, creating a unique print run with your company logo on the cover, or including your company message from a leader in your organisation as the foreword at the front of the book, an additional chapter or case study or a photos section.

It's a very unique and thoughtful gift for your customers and a great way to let them know that your business cares about them.

Media requests

Kate is a sought-after media commentator and is a regular in print, radio, podcasts and on television. As a seasoned speaker and an authority in her space, she is very comfortable talking on topics including:

- The Life List

- Goal Setting and Goal Smashing

- Time Management

- Productivity

- How to find an extra 30+ hours a month

- Work/Life integration

- Women in business

- Impression management

Email Kate: kc@katechristie.com.au.

Printed and bound by CPI Group (UK) Ltd, Croydon, CR0 4YY

13/04/2023

03210417-0001